The Islamic Veil
A Beginner's Guide

Elizabeth Bucar

ONEWORLD

A Oneworld Paperback Original

Published by Oneworld Publications 2012

ISBN 978-1-85168-928-6
eBook ISBN 978-1-78074-097-3

Typeset by Cenveo Publisher Services, Bangalore, India
Cover design by vaguelymemorable.com

Printed and bound in Great Britain by
TJ International, Padstow, Cornwall

Oneworld Publications
185 Banbury Road
Oxford OX2 7AR
England

For my mother, Donna Lyn Rinehart

Contents

Contents

Acknowledgements

This project has its roots in my 2004 fieldwork in Iran, supported by a grant from the University of Chicago's Human Rights Program, and in a course I developed in 2009 with the support of Lloyd International Honors College of the University of North Carolina at Greensboro. Research for this book was supported by generous grants from the University of North Carolina at Greensboro including a Kohler International Travel Award, a Regular Faculty Grant, and the Linda Arnold Carlisle Research Grant from the Women's and Gender Studies program. A semester of research leave from UNCG in 2011 allowed me to devote my energies fulltime to this project. A fellowship from the American Association of University Women (AAUW) supported the final phase of editing.

Elizabeth Barre, Shannon Dunn, Grace Kao, Cybelle McFadden, Irene Oh, Karen Ruffle, Ayla Samli, and Amy Vines gave substantial feedback on drafts of various chapters that helped to improve this work considerably. Fieldwork in Iran would not have been as productive without Roja Fazaeli's advice. Ashiiqa Paramita and Carla Jones were knowledgeable guides to Yogyakarta's Islamic fashion scene. Kecia Ali generously read the whole of the first draft and made incredibly helpful comments and suggestions that I was happy to incorporate. Amy Harris and Michelle Hoppen provided invaluable research assistance, which produced a much better book than I could have alone in the same timeframe.

Finally, I want to thank the staff of Oneworld for their help in producing this Beginner's Guide to the Islamic Veil, especially Novin Doostar, who invited me to write this book, Ruth Deary, for her guidance through the production process, and Dawn Sackett, for her careful copy-editing.

List of figures

Introduction

I should confess that despite the fact that I have agreed to write this Beginner's Guide, I never meant for the practice of religious veiling to occupy any prominent place in my research on gender and Islam. Much of the scholarly work on the Islamic veil has already been done. Historical and ethnographic research has countered older interpretations of the veil as antithetical to modernity. Scholars have eloquently argued that the practice of veiling is a complex one, which is informed by the experience of colonization, nationalization, economic development, and globalization. Similarly, work has been done criticizing the claim that all Muslim women have an obligation to cover themselves. These accounts complicate the conventional view of veiling as merely a sign of the subordination of women. Because I am not myself a veiling Muslim woman, to write another book about the veil might appear to contribute to a pervasive non-Muslim obsession with the veil rather than providing new descriptive or analytical work about it.

Three things thwarted my attempt to avoid writing about the veil. First, the veil continues to hold a prominent place in our understanding of the relationship between religion and politics, and in particular women's freedom. Yet many Muslims, as well as non-Muslims, remain confused about the significance of the Islamic veil. Because I work on gender and Islam, the veil is the topic about which I am most often asked to comment by my students, during public lectures, and even by family and friends. In other words, ignoring the veil is simply not possible for a scholar of gender and Islam in our current geo-political context.

Second, assumptions about the veil have affected my ability to understand the actions of religious women in a cross-cultural context. This first became clear to me in 2004 while I was interviewing leaders of the Iranian women's movement in an attempt to identify their specific goals and strategies in affecting social change. Since Islamic dress is legally required of all women in Iran (see chapter 3), I assumed that the women I would speak with would consider compulsory veiling to be among the top violations of women's rights in Iran. Not only was this not the case (in fact none of the leaders I interviewed considered veiling a significant rights issue in Iran), I also found that, as a whole, leaders of the women's movement wore very conservative dress within the spectrum of their own local practices. In fact, the counter-veiling movement within Iran is not part of the women's rights movement. Instead it is a youth movement tied to the consumption of fashion (see chapter 8).

A final reason for writing this book is that I continue to be frustrated that mainstream discourse about the veil, such as in media reports and political debates, almost always reduces it to a sign of Islamic fundamentalism. Most of the work that struggles against this one-dimensional reading of the veil has been produced by academics strictly for their colleagues. While scholars are often great resources of specialized knowledge about their area of study, we do not always successfully communicate this knowledge to the general public. Thus, this book will translate some of these scholarly conversations for a broader readership interested in thinking critically about what has become a contentious issue in the contemporary world.

My initial misunderstandings of the Iranian veil, which were affected by a specific feminist ideology that I will discuss below, made me realize not only that I want to contribute to the discussion about the veil's role in the religious, moral, and political life of women, but that a comparative study is the ideal way to introduce this subject. In this book I explain the various and changing meanings and power of the Islamic veil in multiple contexts. I hope that understanding the diversity of veiling practices encourages some readers to reevaluate their assumptions about women and Islam.

The Islamic veil is a common subject in media, classrooms, and political debates. However, it is often analyzed in one of two ways: 1) establishing reasons for veiling (e.g. Why do women veil? Do they do so freely?), or 2) assessing whether veiling is 'good' or 'bad' within a specific framework (e.g. international law, secular-liberalism, feminism). This book, however, attempts to do something new. Instead of an exclusive concern with why people veil, or even if they should, I explore why the veil is so prominent in discourse about gender and Islam and how this has altered the lives of contemporary Muslim women who veil. The approach is thoroughly comparative and contextualized, so that the reader can understand how the Islamic veil is active, alive, elastic, and recreated over and over in new ways.

This book is an overview of the Islamic veil rather than a polemic for or against it. I discuss the arguments of others who express why the veil is important to Islam, what the Islamic veil ideally entails, and even why the Islamic veil is unnecessary. I summarize these arguments to help the reader understand the range of debate about the veil, not to persuade that any one of these positions is correct. This is not to say that this book is completely objective. I have a dog in the fight too. My argument is against discourses that reduce the veil to a mere symbol or homogenize this extraordinarily diverse practice. The one conclusion I hope every reader reaches by the end of this book is that there is simply no consensus on the meaning of the Islamic veil. In response to the question, 'Why do Muslim women veil?' we should always ask for clarification. What women do you mean? Where are they veiling? In front of whom? What are the local cultural and historical expectations of veiling? How has veiling been tied to local politics? And so on. The face-veil of

Egypt in 1900 (see chapter 4) is not the same as the 'new veil' of women in Turkey in the 1990s (see chapter 6) or the post-9/11 veil in the US (see chapter 7), or the emerging Indonesian fashion veil (see chapter 8). In each of those cases the reason women veil is different, as is the manner in which others perceive their veiling. To understand the complexity of the Islamic veil, I ask a wide range of questions throughout this book, including: What do Islamic sacred texts and law say about the veil? In what ways have colonialism, nationalism, and Islamic movements affected the Islamic veil? How does veiling affect employment opportunities for Muslim women? In which ways is it used as a symbol of identity? When is the Islamic veil also a fashion statement? How has the veil affected not only Muslim women who cover, but also those who do not? The veil can never exist in a vacuum of pure doctrine so its social, cultural, historical, and economic contexts must be as much the point of study as the veil itself.

The 'Islamic veil' and new geographies of terminology

The word *veil* has Latin roots (*velum*), although the practice of covering the head and body with cloth is even older. As early as 3000 BCE, for instance, Mesopotamian women covered their heads and bodies. The Hebrew Bible has a number of references to head and face-veils (e.g. Genesis 24:64–65 and Isaiah 47:2), which suggests that women of ancient Babylonia and Judea veiled. Middle Assyrian Law (c. 1300 BCE) contains the oldest known statute about regulating women's veiling. Clause 40 requires women who were not prostitutes or slaves to cover their head in public; clause 41 requires a man who wanted to marry his concubine to physically veil her in front of witnesses. In ancient Athens (500–323 BCE), respectable women were, for the most part, secluded within the household and covered in public.

Roman women were not secluded, but they did wear large rectangular shawls called *palla*. Inscriptions on coins show us that women in the Achaemenid (550–330 BCE) and Sasanian empires (224–651) veiled as a form of adornment. Later, according to the New Testament (1 Corinthians 11:4–15), some Christian churches requested women to cover their heads. The evidence of veils and gender segregation in many regions and societies challenges the myth that the veil represents the core of Muslim difference.

In its title and throughout this book I use the term Islamic veil to refer to a cluster of ideas, debates, and practices about modest Muslim dress that includes the covering of at least some head hair. The choice of this term, and the provisional definition of it, is done reluctantly, especially since the main purpose of this book is to resist the temptation to reduce the veil to one of its various (political, material, or theological) dimensions, or to declare that there is a singular thing called an Islamic veil. I have even avoided linking the veil expressly to Muslim women since we have cases of Muslim men who also veil, including the Prophet Muhammad (see chapter 2) and the Tuareg men of Morocco who wear turbans and face-veils (see chapter 6). In addition, the term veil has no exact referent in Arabic, and thus risks appearing to be a Western, scholarly invention. Nevertheless, it is necessary to settle on a term that can help guide us through a comparative and historical introduction to the subject.

One reason to settle on Islamic veil is that the alternatives are even more problematic. Veil is used instead of 'headscarf' because in many practices the Islamic veil is not merely a head covering, but rather an entire form of dress including everything from long tunics to bathing suits. In other contexts the Islamic veil can refer to a set of behaviors beyond dress (e.g. sexual modesty or shyness). Simply titling this book *A Beginner's Guide to The Veil* would unfairly privilege the Islamic form of veiling over other cultural or religious practices of head covering, for example a bride's wedding headpiece or an orthodox Jewish woman's wig. This makes the modifier 'Islamic' important, and even when I refer simply to the veil in this book, Islamic is implied. I use Islamic instead of 'Muslim' because Muslims do not construct the veil's meanings in isolation. We will see that non-Muslim ideas about Islam, even erroneous ones, have also influenced the discourse, practice, and meaning of the Islamic veil. The veil is therefore not an object that purely reflects Muslim culture, politics, or religious ideals. That said, what holds these sartorial practices together is that they are all performed by Muslims and tied to Islam both by the practitioners and by those who observe them. I occasionally use veils in the plural in order to remind the reader that this subject is polyvalent: this book is an introduction to not one object (e.g. a headscarf), but rather to a range of forms of Islamic dress, behaviors, and norms that are regionally and historically varied and constantly changing even within the same context.

There are over one billion Muslims in the world today, so of course the term 'Islamic veil' will not mean the same thing to all of them. Some reject this term because of its Western origins; others reject it because they think it implies face-veiling, which does not describe the majority of Muslim veiling practices either historically or today. If this term is not completely satisfactory, however, popular modern usage of Arabic alternatives like *hijab*, *jilbab*, and *khimar* are even more problematic for discussing the Islamic veil from a comparative and historical perspective. *Hijab* is probably the most popular, and certainly in British and American contexts the most common term for Muslim women's dress in the academy. In Jordan, however, *hijab* means only headscarf; in Iran it refers to a woman's entire style of Islamic dress (often a headscarf and overcoat); and in still other contexts it would mean just the long overcoat. Finally, and as we will discuss in detail in chapter 2, when *hijab* is mentioned in the Qur'an, it does not refer to women's dress at all. More accurate for a book on Islamic clothing would be one of the other Arabic terms found in the Qur'an: *jilbab* and *khimar*. The problem with relying on these terms is that they simply have too much geographic variability in modern use. *Khimar* refers in some regions to a face-veil, in others, such as many Gulf states and North Africa, to a headscarf. Indonesians use *jilbab* to refer generally to a woman's Islamic dress, but in Algeria *jilbab* refers specifically to covering with one piece of cloth from head to toe.

There are additional regional terms used to refer to specific forms of the Islamic veil. The Persian term *purdah*, for example, in South Asia refers generally to the segregation of men and women but also sometimes more specifically to the physical protection of women from men's gaze. *Niqab* and *burqa* are often used in the Western media's coverage of the Islamic veil. The Afghan *burqa*, which will be familiar to most readers, has a mesh opening for the eyes (see figure 1). *Niqab* entails face-veiling: dress that covers the lower part of the face with only the eyes exposed. But in Yemen and India, *burqa* refers to modern forms of face-veil. Two traditional versions of the veil that may be held by the wearer in specific situations to cover part of the face are the *abaya* of Saudi Arabia and *chador* in Iran and Pakistan (see figure 2). In Indonesia, however, *chador* refers to a style of the veil that includes a *niqab*, which is perhaps why many Indonesians mistakenly think that the majority of Iranians cover their faces. These variations in terminology are probably one reason for confusion among Muslims about the Islamic veil. It is also a reflection of the diversity of dress in various Muslim communities.

Orientalism and feminism: two influential systems of thought

Two strands of thought – orientalism and feminism – have been especially influential in grounding harsh judgments of the Islamic

Figure 1 Two women wearing the Afghan *burqa* in Kabul, Afghanistan

Figure 2 Picnicking in *chador* in Shiraz, Iran

veil as well as the assumption that it is singular and universal. These ideologies are prevalent not only in mainstream culture, but have also influenced how scholars have approached their study of women and Islam in general.

First, a preoccupation with veiling as a sign of patriarchal oppression is an example of what Edward Said has called orientalism. Said defined orientalism as 'a style of thought based upon an ontological and epistemological distinction made between "the Orient" and (most of the time) "the Occident"' (Said 2003, 2–3). This 'ontological distinction' is that the East, and by association Islam, is assumed to be a unified thing that is at its essence different from the West, defined geographically as North America and Europe, and philosophically by secularism and Christianity. One effect of this aspect of orientalism is a perception of the veil as singular and universal since Islam is assumed to be the same everywhere. This has in turn led to a tendency to ignore concrete local historical circumstances of the veil in an impossible quest for the 'true essence' of veiling (for example, in Islamic sacred texts). We will see that one of the most crucial dimensions to understanding the Islamic veil is the manner in which what it means varies tremendously from place to place, time to time, and among different people.

Orientalism's 'epistemological distinction' − a fundamental difference in systems of knowledge − grounds a belief that Islam is more backward than the 'enlightened', 'progressive', and 'civilized' West. This sets up not only an artificial opposition between Islam and modernity, but also a hierarchy: to become civilized, Muslims will need to reject Islamic traditions. This epistemological distinction leads to a judgment of the veil as backwards, and thus as a practice that should eventually be cast off.

The second political and philosophical construct that inhibits our ability to understand the Islamic veil is, perhaps ironically, feminism. Feminism is a commitment to eradicating oppression of people based on sex and gender. Often, feminism is concerned with women being empowered in their lives. The problem is that feminism has historically run the risk of treating women in different cultural contexts as if they had the same desires and goals as white middle-class Western women. This simultaneously creates a hierarchy between women and homogenizes the experience of all women (note how similar this effect is to orientalism's in that both perceive the veil as monolithic and judge the veil harshly).

Despite the well-meaning intentions of feminists, particular types of feminism (especially secular feminism of the late twentieth and early twenty-first centuries) can be quick to judge all Muslim women as oppressed. In this logic, the veil is the ultimate symbol and tool of oppression of Muslim women by Muslim men, and veiled women are the betrayers of women's rights for submitting to their own oppression. This feminist framework dismisses Muslim women who declare they freely choose the Islamic veil: these women are seen to be illogical or brainwashed, and the ultimate proof is the fact that they are veiled, since no free woman would do so (see, for instance, the discussion of Egypt in chapter 4 and of France in chapter 6).

Many readers of this Beginner's Guide will initially share these sorts of feminist commitments, and in fact this sort of feminism is what originally attracted me to the study of gender and Islam. This does not, however, mean that ultimately we cannot understand and respect a mode of being which is different from our own. In fact, what is so interesting from a feminist point of view is how studying women different from ourselves can push us to rethink the content and scope of our own feminist commitments. In other words, we can learn not to judge a veil as oppressive unless the particular circumstances of a veiled woman demonstrate that it is. In some of the cases discussed in this book, for instance, women argue that their veil is a symbol of feminist protest (see in particular veils in the workplace in chapter 5 and as expressions of identity in chapter 7).

Chapter overview

This book is organized into eight thematic chapters. The first three chapters provide an overview of the sources and arguments about a Muslim woman's duty to veil in traditional sources (Qur'an, hadith, and law) and modes of Islamic thinking (ethics, textual interpretation, legal reasoning). The remaining five chapters each consider a different historical event or dimension of life in which the Islamic veil has taken on a particular significance. These chapters will draw from ethnographically and historically informed sources in order to demonstrate the diversity of meanings and practices of Islamic veiling in a variety of countries (Afghanistan, Algeria, Egypt, France, India, Indonesia, Iran, Morocco, Palestine, Saudi Arabia, Tajikistan, Turkey, the United Kingdom, and the United States). Case studies will include the new veiling movements among middle class women in Egypt; the role of the veil in American Muslim identity post-9/11; and the emergence of fashion-veiling in post-Suharto Indonesia. By employing a number of regionally diverse case studies, this book takes a global and comparative perspective on the issue of veiling, thus demonstrating its variations and complexities.

Chapter 1, Ethics, introduces the range of moral issues related to the veil. It is no surprise that for proponents of veiling modesty is its main justification. But moral concerns rarely stop at the level of individual piety, especially since piety is enacted in relation to other people as well as for the good of the community. This means that the ethics of veiling are socially and historically situated and influenced by other phenomena and agendas. Chapter 1 provides a short primer on Muslim ethics as a subfield of Islamic studies. It proposes three ways to frame the ethics of the veil (personal, interpersonal, and social ethics), and uses an anecdote of my own experience with temporary veiling to demonstrate the ethical power of the Islamic veil.

Chapter 2, Sacred texts, analyzes what the Qur'an and hadith, important textual sources of Islamic revelation, say about the veil. This chapter provides an overview of the challenges to interpreting these texts, which is by no means an easy or straight-forward process of reading. I describe the three Qur'anic revelations that are most often cited by proponents and critics of the veil. These three verses contain tremendous diversity, especially in regards to what the veil is, who has a duty to veil, and for what reason they must veil. This leaves them open to a wide range of interpretations.

Chapter 3, Law, describes the manner in which legal reasoning has influenced the development of the Islamic veil. The chapter begins with an introduction to the texts, institutions, sources, and methods of Islamic legal thinking in order to show how Islamic law is fundamentally a system of diversity and change. Medieval jurists had an especially large impact on our current perception of the Islamic veil by linking female bodies to general disorder (*fitna*). Three cases in which veiling became nationally required (Iran, Saudi Arabia, Afghanistan) demonstrate the impact of Islamic law on modern legal codes.

Chapter 4, Colonialism, considers how the Islamic veil gains new significance during the colonization of majority Muslim populations. This is an important example of how the meaning of the veil is not solely determined by the development of Islamic thought in isolation, but rather through concrete interactions of Muslims with non-Muslims, and in turn, the interaction of local and foreign discourses about religion, gender, and modernity. Three cases studies (Egypt, Algeria, and Palestine) consider how foreign ideologies and occupations affect local veiling practices. Colonizers who interpreted veiling as a sign of underdevelopment greatly increased the local political importance of the Islamic veil. Even in areas where veiling was not popular nor necessarily linked to Islam before occupation, nationalist movements that resisted foreign occupation and rule adopted the veil as the symbol of their political resistance.

Chapter 5, Employment, focuses on how veiling influences Muslim women's access to employment opportunities. In recent decades, economic development in Muslim majority countries has increased the demand for Muslim women to work outside the home. Although Islam does support women's economic rights, these rights can be perceived to be in tension with the importance placed on a woman as the center of the family unit and primary caregiver to children. In some cases (Egypt), women have successfully used the veil to communicate a continued commitment to Islamic gender ideology even as they enter the workforce. In other contexts (the United States), veiling has been a source of discrimination in the workplace. Legal challenges to this discrimination have more often than not been unsuccessful.

Chapter 6, Education, explains the recent heated debates about young women's veiling in educational institutions. National policies range from requiring veiling in schools, to barring veiled girls from registering altogether. What these cases have in common is that the Islamic veil has begun to determine whether Muslim girls can obtain an education. This chapter will look at the well-known cases of the French and Turkish bans on headscarves in schools, as well as the lesser-known policies on Islamic veils in Tajikistan and Indonesia. In these contexts, the veil has become entangled with concerns over the influence of political Islam, the stability of secular republics, and the role of religious freedom in increasingly religiously plural countries.

Chapter 7, Identity, argues that the Islamic veil is sufficiently complex to convey various types of identity. Three categories of identity are discussed – ascribed, chosen, and declared – in order to complicate the notion of the identity of a veiled individual beyond merely 'a Muslim woman'. The case of Muslim Berber men who veil shows how the veil can convey an ascribed identity that is male gendered. First generation immigrants who begin veiling after moving to the UK, or second-generation British youth who veil over the protests of their families, are examples of a chosen hybrid cultural identity. Post-9/11, the Islamic veil becomes an important symbol of American Muslim identity when it is adopted as a symbol of protest against Islamophobia.

Chapter 8, Fashion, considers how Muslim women who veil adopt, challenge, and set fashion trends. Islamic veils have many meanings, but they are also part of some Muslim women's sartorial practices. Fashionable Islamic dress includes both articles specifically produced and marketed to Muslim women as 'up-to-date', as well as women's styling of non-specialized clothing to abide by Islamic covering recommendations. Three case studies of fashionable veiling are explored in order to show the effect of fashion on the Islamic principles behind veiling. In Iran, for example, young girls who wear what is locally called *bad hijab* influence how Iranian laws requiring veiling are enforced. In Indonesia, the recent popularity of fashion-veiling has been justi-fied by linking aesthetics with ethics, and thus outer beauty with inner piety. Both Muslim and Hindu South Indian women wear saris, but they style them differently. This variation in fashion demonstrates multiple understandings of what is required for modest women's dress.

1
Ethics

We are all ethicists. We grapple with what makes an action right or wrong, what makes a person virtuous or not, and what makes a society good or bad. While certainly not the only source of ethical systems for determining what is moral, religions have been key to shaping our reflections on these issues. Islam is no exception. Although there is no agreement among Muslims about the ethics of veiling, ethical debates are part of the story of the Islamic veil.

In everyday usage, the terms ethics and morality are often used interchangeably. Technically, morality is what people actually believe and do – our ideas about what is right and wrong, good and bad, which guide our actions and judgments of others – while ethics is the intellectual reflection on this morality. There is no exact cognate for 'ethics' in the Islamic intellectual tradition. *Akhlaq*, the Qur'anic term used to refer to the prophet Muhammad's moral character, and *adab*, proper conduct or manners, are good parallels insofar as they have to do with correct behavior and virtue.

Islamic ethics draws on many sources including the Qur'an and the moral example set by the Prophet and his companions, referred to as the Sunna and recorded in traditions called the hadith. A Muslim living today has access not only to written sources for ethics, but to a long tradition of interpretation of these sources in various forums, some of which will be the focus of other chapters of this volume (e.g. sacred texts in chapter 2 and law in chapter 3). In developing ethical thought Muslims have also engaged in vigorous intellectual debate and interacted with various other ethical traditions, including Greek, Persian,

Indian, Jewish, and Christian. In addition, Muslim believers make judgments and act out of a sense of what is moral everyday. This means part of the content of Islamic ethics is what, how, and why Muslims see certain actions as having particular moral meanings.

A couple of general principles of Islamic ethics will help orient the reader. First, Islamic ethics emphasizes norms like human dignity, justice, compassion, mercy, and duty to one's family life. In terms of ethical reflection on the veil, chastity, dignity, shyness, obedience, femininity, and modesty are all common normative concerns. Second, Islam has no concept equivalent to Christianity's 'original sin'. The assumption is that humans are able to 'be good', even if the moral life (what is sometimes referred to as following the 'straight path') is difficult. Third, Islam teaches that each person has moral agency (Qur'an 81:28, 82:5) and therefore is responsible, and ultimately accountable, for his or her own deeds on the Last Day of Judgment. Finally, Islamic ethics is not just a moral code for right action. There is also a deep interest in how right action can make virtuous Muslims, strengthen relationships, and contribute to a just and stable society.

From one perspective, this entire book is about the ethical meaning of the Islamic veil, as shaped through traditional sources and modes of reasoning (chapters 2 and 3), historical events (chapter 4), or within specific dimensions of daily life (chapters 5, 6, 7, and 8). This chapter describes some general ways ethicists frame discussions about the meaning and power of the Islamic veil and attempts to translate some of these frameworks for the non-specialist in a more general way. To help organize these frameworks, I identify three types of ethical issues at stake for the Islamic veil, that have to do with moral issues in personal, interpersonal, and social arenas of life. Personal ethics involves a focus on how everyday practices, repeated over time, are part of an individual's ethical formation. The veil, from the personal ethical perspective, has a role in forming the character and inner dispositions of Muslim women. Interpersonal ethics is concerned with relationships, including sexual relations between men and women. Within the interpersonal ethical rubric the veil is analyzed in terms of its effects on sexual norms between men and women, especially how it strengthens marital bonds and prevents immoral sexual desires. Social ethics looks at appropriate behavior for people as a whole and considers the veil's impact on wider society.

Personal ethics: character formation through bodily acts

A good place to begin to understand how veiling creates a certain sort of person is with the significance of practices to Muslim ethics. The technical term for the emphasis on correct practices is *orthopraxy* in contrast with *orthodoxy*, which emphasizes correct belief. Certainly we can see the importance of practice in the five pillars of Islam – pilgrimage, alms-giving, prayer, witness of faith, and ritual fasting. This is not to say that Islam has no place for beliefs, but rather that we must also consider the meanings and effects of the physical actions of Muslims as well.

When scholars talk to each other about the ways actions affect the people who do them they almost always reference French philosophers like Michel Foucault or Pierre Hadot. These thinkers write about the manner in which bodily actions, which they categorize as 'technologies of the self' (Foucault 1990) and 'spiritual exercises' (Hadot 1995), affect who a person is. This is not just an existential claim such as 'you are what you do' or 'you are the sum of your actions'. Rather the core idea is that practices modify and transform a person who performs them.

The role of bodily practice in moral formation is crucial for understanding why some women veil, as well as how veiling affects them. This view of the moral life assumes that in order for a woman to be moral, she must do the right things. Think of a musician who logs in hours of daily practice in order to hone her craft. Some Muslims see veiling as a type of 'practice' that builds the skills necessary to be successful at being good.

Certain actions are also associated with specific virtues. If you do something often enough, these virtues are 'imprinted' on you. For the Islamic veil these virtues might include modesty, shyness, or obedience. During Saba Mahmood's research on Egyptian Muslim women one of her informants describes a connection between veiling and becoming shy:

> It's just like the veil. In the beginning when you wear it, you're embarrassed and don't want to wear it because people say that you look older and unattractive, that you won't get married and will never find a husband. But you must wear the veil, first because it is God's command and then, with time, because your inside learns to feel shy without the veil, and if you take it off, your entire being feels uncomfortable about it (Mahmood 2005, 157).

Gaining shyness is not the extension of one's initial tendencies, but a process of acquiring norms through bodily actions. Eventually the women come to feel shy spontaneously and want to wear the veil.

In traditional Islamic thought this change is described by the Arabic word *malaka* (habit or habitus). The medieval Islamic philosopher Ibn Khaldun describes *malaka* as 'a firmly rooted quality acquired by doing a certain action and repeating it time after time, until the form of that action is firmly fixed' in the disposition of a person (Ibn Khaldun 1958, 346). The idea is that specific actions, such as wearing a veil, are repeated as part of a program of moral training. That these actions are difficult is part of the point. In the beginning, veiling is hard. It takes a conscious effort. But after time, a woman acquires *malaka* so that she wants to veil and unveiling is what feels uncomfortable.

This role of practice in character formation should help shift us from seeing the veil only as a symbol (of piety, submission, identity) to seeing it as the means by which virtues are made. On the one hand this is a connection of inner and outer dimensions of the human life. The veil is not merely clothing, it is intimately linked to one's inner orientation and spiritual development. On the other hand, the veil is not only the marker of piety or modesty: it is itself part of what defines piety. This is why bans on the veil are so egregious to some Muslims: they can be interpreted as taking away a woman's ability to *be* and even *become* pious.

Interpersonal ethics: regulating sexual desires between men and women

Interpersonal ethics refers to those aspects of ethics that deal with issues arising from our relationships with other people. Unlike personal ethics, which is concerned mainly with the actions and virtues of individuals, and social ethics, which considers the moral life of the wider social unit, the interpersonal dimension of ethics looks at what is acceptable and desirable in our interactions with friends, family, and even strangers. For the Islamic veil, the interpersonal ethics most discussed are those concerned with human sexuality, such as the effect of women's bodies on men and the danger of immoral sexual encounters.

In general, Islam sees human sexuality as positive: it both acknowledges sex as a human need and as potentially embodying virtues such as kindness, reciprocity, and generosity. Within the context of a legal marriage, spouses even have a right to sexual satisfaction that is independent of procreative aims (Ali 2006, 7). Islam teaches that sexual intimacy is an important part of a full human life.

Nonetheless, Islam does not support sexual anarchy or teach that sex is good under all circumstances. Specifically, moral sexual activity is limited to a legally married man and woman. In current ethical discourse, the term *zina* (which will be discussed more in chapters 2 and 3) is used to refer to illicit sex between unmarried partners. Sex is therefore good, because it is crucial for a fully human life, but morally regulated, because it is powerful and therefore potentially dangerous. Two of the most commonly discussed dangers are the chaos created by women's sexuality and the insatiability of men's sexual desire.

Veiling allows, in theory, for the power of human sexuality to be directed only towards its ethical goals in two ways. First, the public veiling of women is meant to prevent inappropriate sexual desires between men and women. It is best to separate unmarried men and women, but strict gender segregation is difficult, if not impossible, and the Islamic veil is a way separation is at least partially enacted. In this way, the veil acts as a mobile honor zone, protecting the honor of the woman no matter where she goes (Okkenhaug & Flaskerud 2005, 126). Second, veiling is meant to strengthen the marital bond by keeping a woman's sensuality for her husband. As Iranian Ayatollah Murtaza Mutahhari (d. 1979) argued in the late 1960s, keeping sex for marriage allows one spouse to be 'the cause for the wellbeing of the other'. He contrasts this to complete sexual freedom, where one's spouse 'gets in the way of that person's "fun" like a prison guard' and the family becomes resented (Mutahhari 1992, 14).

Social ethics: ensuring public dignity and making Islamic spaces

Social ethics is concerned with how a society should act as a whole. Here the concern is less with the behavior of individuals or even interactions between individuals, and more with the appropriate behavior of the collective. A classic example of Islamic social ethics is Abu Nasr Muhammad al-Farabi's (d. 905/951) *al-madinah al-fadilah* (*The Excellent City*, 1906), which explores social ideals produce the greatest good for a city's citizens. Examples of issues taken up by social ethicists are abortion, war, work, and a range of bio-medical issues.

Islamic social ethics reflects on the collective experience of Muslims, both in Muslim majority contexts and in contexts where Muslims are a minority. Since these social contexts are very different, what is moral in one may not necessarily be appropriate for another. Nevertheless, there are certain strands of Islamic social ethics that have been especially influential in debates around the Islamic veil, such as reflections on the impact of sexual desires on the social unit. The Pakistani Islamic leader, Said Abul A'la Maududi (d. 1979) thought 'the most important problem of social life' is 'how to regulate the sexual urge into a system and prevent it from running wild' (Maududi 1972, 141). The veil is offered as a way to regulate these urges for the benefit of society.

Arguments made in support of the veil within this area of ethical reflection often claim that the veil can do four types of things for society. First, some suggest that the veil can prevent men from being constantly aroused and distracted by women's sexuality in public places. By hiding the more alluring parts of a woman's body from view, such as her hair and her bosom, the Islamic veil in theory creates a sexually sanitized social space. This protects what Mutahhari refers to as 'social dignity'. The 'tranquility of the spirit of society', he argues, demands 'that a man and a woman choose a special way of relating to each other' (Mutahhari 1992, 42).

Second, some argue the veil encourages economic productivity by visually segregating women and men so they are not distracted by their sexual desires for each other. Simply put, the workers will be able to get more done when they are not busy flirting or staring at each other lustfully. The same is said about places of learning, where boys and girls are assumed to listen, learn, and think better when not distracted by their raging hormones.

Third, some supporters of the veil think it allows Muslim women to more fully participate in society by protecting their modesty as well as their physical safety. If every woman veils the entire public sphere becomes an Islamic honor zone, and thus morally safe for Muslim women.

Finally, the veil is seen as a way to prevent social immorality by guarding women from external, especially Western, immoral influences. Through much of the twentieth and twenty-first centuries, many Islamic leaders have been concerned with undoing the effects of Western socialization, which they believe distort Islamic culture and values. Women are seen as especially vulnerable to Western infection, which some Islamists claim deprives women of their chastity, modesty, and honor. The Islamic veil is posited as one antidote for this social infection. In chapters 3 and 4, for instance, we will see that some Muslim leaders argued that public un-veiling was a cause of widespread social demise and immoral behavior and that public re-veiling would be necessary to establish social harmony.

Ethical critiques of the Islamic veil

This book is primarily an attempt to describe and explain the reasons why women veil and the power of this veiling in different dimensions of life. However it is helpful to point out some of the ethical critiques that are made about Islamic veiling so that the reader is not left with the impression that all Islamic ethical thought supports the veil.

In terms of the personal arguments for veiling, critics point out that it is a gross reduction of the full meaning of piety and modesty when they are linked too closely with the veil. Reducing piety to the veil for women is a flattening of a much broader personal process of character formation that occurs throughout one's daily life. In terms of modesty, a headscarf can actually increase a woman's beauty (as discussed in chapter 8 on fashion). Many women who wear the veil also use makeup. Other women enact modesty without the veil. For many Muslims, real modesty is an attitude, not a form of dress, marked by the avoidance of alluring looks, or flirtatious laughs. The nineteenth-century Muslim reformer Jamal al-Din al-Afghani (d. 1897) defined modesty as resistance of doing sinful actions (translated in Moazzam 1984, 78). More recently, the progressive Islamic leader Muhammad Said Ashmawi (b. 1932) argued, 'the real meaning of *hijab* lies in thwarting the self from straying toward lust or illicit desires, and keeping away from sinful behavior, without having to conjoin this [understanding] with particular forms of clothing and attire' (translated by Mahmood 2005, 160).

Critics of Islamic veiling also comment within the realm of interpersonal ethics. They argue that the veil is neither necessary nor sufficient to prevent illicit sexual desires. A man and woman can still flirt, or commit 'adultery of the eyes' (Maududi 1972, 180), even if the woman is wearing a veil. Others have argued that the Islamic veil is just as likely to create desire as to prevent it by marking women's bodies as forbidden: cultural studies scholar Faegheh Shirazi has shown, for instance, how common stereotypes of the exoticism and sensuality of veiled women are used in Western advertisements (Shirazi 2001, 39–61). Finally, although the Qur'anic directives about sexual modesty considered in chapter 2 address both men and women, the current emphasis on women's modest dress in the form of the veil neglects men's role in interpersonal sexual ethics. In fact it seems to be men's unruly desire that makes women's bodies so troubling to sexual ethics in the first place. Sociologist Marnia Lazreg has argued that when men say the veil protects against sexual harassment, what they are really doing is giving themselves permission to act badly. She equates it to taking an aspirin every night to prevent a heart attack. 'It's a step that one takes', she argues, 'so that when a heart attack occurs, one can always say, "I did all the right things"' (Lazreg 2009, 51).

Finally, some critiques of veiling can be categorized as arguments from within social ethics. Social reasons are often used to justify compulsory veiling of all women as the only way to guarantee a socially Islamic space. Critics of veiling, however, point out that requiring veiling undermines the ability of veiling to be a conscious virtuous choice: if veiling is mandatory, there is no way to make veiling a personal, moral decision. Others point out that mandatory veiling collapses a distinction in Islam between religion (*din*) and life (*dunia*). Muslim women do not devote every aspect of their daily lives to the worship of God. That would be equating Muslim veiling to a Catholic nun's habit (as nuns do in fact devote their lives to religion). Women's other daily tasks, cooking, cleaning, working, caring, in no way lessen their commitment to Muslim ethics, but these mundane activities are not themselves religious or necessarily moral (Lazreg 2009, 25). A woman can be pious, these critics argue, without having a religious or ethical motivation for every daily task.

Summary: the ethical impact of my temporary veiling

In the summer of 2004, I lived in Tehran, Iran, studying Persian and conducting research. Although I am not Muslim, like every other woman in Iran, I was required to veil in public, and so I did. Most of the time I wore a headscarf and a short coat-like garment called a *manteau*. When I visited Shi'i shrines, I wore a long black *chador* that covered everything but my face.

For me, veiling was not part of a conscious attempt to be Muslim or more modest around men. I never intended it to affect me in any way. My Islamic dress was simply obedience to the national laws and respect for the customs of my host country. At first I felt awkward veiled. It was like dressing up in some exotic costume: sort of silly, a little embarrassing.

However, it did not take long for me to get used to the veil. A favorite break from my studies quickly became shopping for new scarves. I began to notice and admire the subtle differences in women's veils. Despite the fact that the temperature was often above 90 degrees, I did not feel Islamic clothing made me more physically uncomfortable. Had you asked me a month into my stay, I would have said I had become used to 'dressing up' in the veil and that the veil was no big deal after all. At that point, I did not think the Islamic veil had affected me, my interactions with others, or my expectations for the social sphere in any meaningful ways.

When I left Iran, I spent a few weeks in Turkey before returning home to the United States. Veiling is optional in Turkey and it would seem odd for a non-Muslim woman to cover her hair in a city like Istanbul, so I did not. I immediately felt exposed without my veil. I could not imagine wearing a tank top or strappy dresses that would have been my normal uniform in the summer in the US. But my new attitude was not only about my own dress. I was shocked by the tighter and brighter versions of the veil in Turkey. They seemed 'improper'. I had also come to expect certain things from interactions with strange men. I found myself offended when Turkish men would touch my hand or even hold eye contact when giving me change, both of which are considered rude in Iran where men and women try not to touch in public. I noted that the Turkish public space was not as sexually regulated as in Iran. I was suddenly more conscious of being a woman traveling alone.

My point is not that a couple of months of veiling had 'made me Muslim' or 'moral' but merely that veiling did affect the way I saw myself, the way I interacted with others, and my expectations for how the social space should be organized. Veiling had ethically transformed me, even if just a little.

2
Sacred texts

Proponents and critics of the Islamic veil alike quote sacred texts to support their positions. When asked why they cover their head, body, or face, most Muslim women reply that they are following a written directive in Islamic scripture. And when someone asks, 'What is the Islamic origin of veiling?', more often than not what they want to know is what the sacred texts say on the issue. An introduction to the Islamic veil would not be complete without a chapter devoted to the sacred texts, and we have two such texts to consider: the Qur'an and the hadith.

One reason for the prominence of Islamic sacred texts in contemporary debates over the veil is that in the last 100 years global Islamic revivalist movements have turned to these texts to find solutions to what are perceived as modern threats to Islam from, for instance, colonialism (see chapter 4) or secularism (see chapter 6). Within the Muslim community there are a range of approaches to sacred texts, which Islamic studies scholar Barbara Freyer Stowasser groups in three broad categories: modernist, traditionalist, and fundamentalist. Fundamentalists have been especially influential in politicizing sacred texts as they insist on literal interpretations and applications to modern situations (Stowasser 1994, 6–7). Influenced by the writings of contemporary Islamic leaders such as Hassan al-Banna (d. 1949), Said Qutb (d. 1966), and Maududi (d. 1979), this strand of scriptural activism conceives sacred texts as timeless rulebooks and obedience to them as a requirement for any authentic Islamic discourse. There is a danger to privileging sacred texts as sources of religious authority in this way, especially since feminist scholars have convincingly argued that the interpretation of textual Islam has been, for the most part, under the control of the male elite (Mernissi 1991). Nevertheless, these texts continue to influence how Muslims understand right practice. In this chapter we explore the nuance, complexity, and ambiguity of what these texts say about the Islamic veil.

Our first step is to understand what the Qur'an and hadith are, how they were originally transmitted, when they were codified, and methods of their interpretation. Muslims regard the Qur'an as the verbatim record of God's word revealed in Arabic to the Prophet Muhammad over twenty-three years, from 610 to 632. Although Muslims accept prior revelation (e.g. Bible, Torah) and Prophets (e.g. Abraham, Noah, and Jesus), they understand these earlier divine instructions to be incomplete and corrupted by humans. The Qur'an is God's last revelation, sent to correct all that had been misunderstood, and to complete God's message to the world.

Qur'an in Arabic means *recital*, and the oral dimension of the Qur'an is key to its nature: Muhammad received and shared the Qur'an orally, the early Muslim community spread the Qur'an orally, and today the Qur'an continues to function as an oral text, through ritual recitation. The Qur'an's Arabic is very special, even to the ear of a native Arabic speaker, and has much in common with pre-Islamic forms of poetry. The written Arabic text we have today, comprised of 114 chapters (*suwar*, sing. *sura*) of various verses (*ayat*, sing. *aya*), was collected within a few years of the Prophet's death by Uthman ibn Affan (d. 656) who ruled as the third Caliph. Most Muslims accept this written version as the authentic and exact replica of revelation.

The Qur'an is available in English translation. In this book, I provide two translations of key verses. The first translation is Arthur Arberry's, a well-respected version often assigned in introductory college courses on Islam (Arberry 1996). The second translation provided is Yusuf Ali's, a popular version which is used in many Muslim homes (Ali 2010). Neither is perfect, and each has its own exegetical assumptions, which is why for the non-Arabic reader, consulting multiple translations is important. For readers of Arabic, I suggest consulting N. J. Dawood's version, which has the advantage of including a parallel Arabic text (Dawood 2006).

Since the primary purpose of this chapter is to explain how the sacred texts serve as a source for veiling, I do not delve into theological debates about the created versus uncreated nature of the Qur'an. In other words, the analysis that follows assumes that the Qur'an is uncreated, divine, eternal speech because that is how the majority of Muslims view this text. This view of the Qur'an as 'uncreated' means that although it was revealed during a specific historical time period of the Prophet's life, Muhammad was not the author of the text, nor is his life understood to drive the process of its formulation.

The discipline of Qur'anic exegesis (*tafsir*) developed to explain the Qur'an's norms and teachings to Muslims. This interpretive work is necessary because although the Qur'an is the primary source for how to live a pious Muslim life, its difficult, obscure, and poetic language is not easy to apply to human lives. *Tafsir* is a place where significantly diverse understandings of Islam emerge because the process of interpretation takes place in concrete social, economic, and political situations, where other forms of knowledge and practical concerns are necessarily put into conversation with the sacred text. It is also important to note that even early Qur'anic commentaries were written after Muhammad's death, when veiling was already a customary practice. This undoubtedly affected how the Qur'an was read on this issue.

Although most Muslims will cite specific verses from the Qur'an as justification for the Islamic veil, there is surprisingly little scholarship available in English that explores the interpretive challenges of these verses. Notable exceptions are listed in the further reading section at the end of this book. In this chapter, I loosely follow the 'traditionalist' practice of Qur'anic exegesis (as Stowasser defines it) and consider relevant verses phrase-by-phrase and word-by-word. For particular key concepts, I discuss the root meanings of the Arabic word, as well the word's usage in other parts of the Qur'an. The goal is to disentangle modern meanings from those meanings that would have been more common during the time of the revelations. For the non-Arabic speaker, I plead for patience for the number of transliterated terms in this chapter. To truly understand the debates over specific verses some attention to etymology must be part of our discussion.

Hadith became an important scriptural source, second only to the Qur'an, after the death of the Prophet. Based on oral traditions passed down by word of mouth, hadith are reports of things the Prophet Muhammad said or did. They are used by Muslims to help 'fill in' where Qur'anic revelation is silent. By the eighth and ninth centuries, multi-volume collections of hadith materials were gathered by scholars with the purpose of removing false hadith, invented to serve some political or social purpose, from the tradition. As a result, there are six canonical texts recognized by Sunnis as sound (*sahih*). Contemporary scholars have argued that even these canonical texts reflect the biases and assumptions of their collectors. These biases can be seen, for instance, in how the traditions are arranged, making some seem more reliable than others, and in the sub-headings provided, allowing collectors to guide the reader to specific interpretations (Clarke 2003).

The political break between Sunni and Shi'a is discussed in the next chapter, but for the purposes of this chapter it is important to note that Shi'i hadiths also include the sayings and doings of the Imams, who led the Shi'i community after the Prophet's death. Shi'i hadith collections are therefore larger and less defined than Sunni ones, and there is little scholarship looking at veiling in the collections available in English. While Shi'i hadith certainly deserve their own devoted study, such a study is outside the scope of this book and therefore I limit myself here to Sunni hadith reports.

Since one of the goals of hadith is to provide Muslims with a record of the customs of the Prophet and the early Muslim community, hadith books contain chapters devoted to clothing. However, as Islamic studies professor L. Clarke demonstrates, few hadith deal with women's modest dress, other than in ritual contexts, or to warn against wearing thin clothing or short hemlines (Clarke 2003, 217–219). An important exception is a report that exists only in Tirmidhi's (d. 892) collection that reads 'Woman is "a shameful thing" [*'awra*]. If she goes out, Satan attempts to control her' (translated by Clarke 2003, 218). *'Awra* is discussed in more detail below, but at this point I want to point out that this hadith, which implies that a woman's entire body should be covered in public, is an isolated case. Despite existence of reports involving the color, thickness, style, and care of men's and women's hair, there is no explicit reference in hadith to covering either the head or the hair (Clarke 2003, 222).

Despite this lack of clear references to women's veiling in the hadith, two things can be learned from hadith to help interpret the relevant Qur'anic verses: chronology and context of revelation. The order in which revelations occurred matters because sometimes specific cases of revelation seem to contradict others. One often cited example is an early and apparently pagan revelation (53:19–20), sometimes referred to as the Satanic Verses, which contradicts the unity of Allah (*tawhid*), a central tenet of Islam (see, for example, 112:1–4 and 6:133). Muslims, however, understand this diversity as a strength, not a weakness, of the Islamic revelation: it allowed Allah to present Islam to the early Muslim community in a way that made it easiest for them to understand and accept. Nevertheless this diversity creates a challenge in interpreting the ethical message of the Qur'an. Medieval interpreters of the Qur'an developed the principle of *naskh*, or abrogation of earlier verses by later ones, in order to deal with this challenge. Hadith reports help us determine how two or more revelations are chronologically related so that later revelations can be read as the elaboration and expansion of earlier ones.

The second thing we learn from the hadith is the occasion of revelation (*asbab al-nuzul*), the circumstances that surrounded the Prophet's reception of a specific revelation. This context helps to explain what sort of intervention the revelation might have been in terms of specific actions it called for and specific norms it encouraged. Some 'fundamentalists' (as Stowasser defines them) have tended to downplay this context, fearful that attention to it will make it look like revelations are responses to specific occasions, thus making historical events the 'occasions for' versus 'occasions of' revelation. My use of hadith here is merely to explore the context within which specific verses are revealed; I do not mean to imply they are causing revelation.

There are three verses commonly cited as Qur'anic evidence of the Islamic veil: 33:53, 33:59–60, and 24:30–31. There is an enormous diversity among these verses, even with the terms that get translated as veil (*hijab, jilbab, khimar*). In addition, who is asked to veil, for what reasons, and in front of whom differs in these verses, which complicates what norms are implied by the Qur'anic directives to cover. I consider each verse, with the help of hadith, in order to decipher how, when read together, they establish the Islamic veil as part of the Islamic way of life.

Verse 33:53: privacy in the home

Verse 33:53, sometimes referred to as 'the verse of the *hijab*', is chronologically the first revelation related to Islamic veiling. Drawing on reports recorded in hadith, there is scholarly consensus that this revelation occurred within five years of the Muslim community's emigration from Mecca to Medina.

Fleeing political persecution and social harassment, they formed a religiously pluralistic community under the leadership of the Prophet. As a result of this emigration, the scope of the Prophet's leadership greatly expanded: he changed from the spiritual leader of a Muslim minority to the political leader of the majority. With this new political authority came enormous demands on the Prophet's time. The hadith describe, for instance, the common occurrence of Muslims seeking advice and favors while visiting the Prophet, often in the private quarters of one of his wives.

Hadith reports tell us the revelation recorded in verse 33:53 occurs after the marriage of the Prophet to Zaynab. A number of wedding guests lingered in Zaynab's house after the wedding celebration, causing the Prophet to become annoyed. The Prophet received the following revelation:

> O believers, enter not the houses of the Prophet, except leave is given you for a meal, without watching for its hour. But when you are invited, then enter; and when you have had the meal, disperse, neither lingering for idle talk; that is hurtful to the Prophet, and he is ashamed before you; but God is not ashamed before the truth. And when you ask his wives for any object, ask them from behind a curtain [*hijab*]; that is cleaner for your hearts and theirs. It is not for you to hurt God's Messenger, neither to marry his wives after him ever; surely that would be, in God's sight, a monstrous thing (Arberry 1996, vol. 2, 127–128).

> O you who believe! Do not enter the Prophet's houses – until leave is given you – for a meal, (and then) not (so early as) to wait for its preparation: but when you are invited, enter; and when you have taken your meal, disperse, without seeking familiar talk. Such (behavior) annoys the Prophet: he is ashamed to dismiss you, but God is not ashamed (to tell you) the truth. And when you ask (his ladies) for anything you want, ask them from before a screen [*hijab*]: that makes for greater purity for

your hearts and for theirs. Nor is it right for you that you should annoy God's Messenger, or that you should marry his widows after him at any time. Truly such a thing is in God's sight an enormity (Ali 2010, 319).

This revelation asks all Muslims to abide by various rules when visiting the Prophet, such as waiting for permission to enter his private quarters, and not lingering after their business is completed. In other words, although the Prophet's family life has to be 'public' insofar as he conducts official religious and political business in his home, this verse establishes basic guidelines of etiquette that allow the Prophet to maintain some level of privacy.

In the second part of the verse the way privacy is maintained is specified: Muslim men are told to address the Prophet's wives with a *hijab* between them. Although *hijab* today is used to refer to the Islamic veil, or even more generally to any form of women's Islamic dress, it has a more generic meaning in the Qur'an. In the other places it is used, *hijab* separates things, such as gods from mortals (42:51), wrong-doers from the righteous (7:46), believers from unbelievers (41:5, 17:45), and light from darkness (38:32). In fact other than verse 33:53, *hijab* refers to women in only one other place in the Qur'an, 19:17, where it partitions Maryam (Mary, mother of Jesus Christ). This means the Qur'anic *hijab* is not necessarily an article of clothing, nor is it tied necessarily to women. At its most basic level, *hijab* in the Qur'an is a term used merely to connote borders and establish thresholds.

In verse 33:53, *hijab* could be interpreted in at least three ways. First, *hijab* can be a visual barrier, hiding something (the Prophet and his wives) from sight. This is most likely Ali's interpretation, since he translates it as 'screen'. This *hijab* makes a visible, symbolic boundary between the Prophet's family and the rest of the community.

Second, *hijab* can be a physical barrier used to partition a space, providing domestic comfort and privacy for the female elite (Stowasser 1994, 91). This coheres with Arberry's translation of 'curtain', and is confirmed by the tradition we have relayed by the Prophet's servant Anas Ibn Malik, in which we learn that not only Zaynab, but also Muhammad, is secluded when the *hijab* is drawn: 'At that time the Verse of *Hijab* was revealed, and he [the Prophet] set a *sitr* [curtain] between him and me' (al-Bukhari, translated in Goto 2004, 283).

A third possible meaning of *hijab* is as an ethical barrier. In verse 33:53 *hijab* is sometimes interpreted as making something forbidden (e.g. the Prophet's wives) based on the fact that the partitioning of space is linked in the verse with a concern for the 'purity of hearts' of both the wives and the Muslim men who visit them. The case for an ethical meaning of *hijab* is further strengthened when we read in a subsequent revelation (33:55) exceptions to the 'screening' of the Prophet's wives from their male relatives and male servants with whom face-to-face interactions presumably do not entail any potentially inappropriate sexual desires. Hadith reports referring to *hijab* assume that its purpose was to prevent not only men looking sinfully at women, but also women looking sinfully at men. For example, a report in both Ibn Sa'ad's (d. 845) and Abu Dawud's (d. 889) collections tells of an instance in which the Prophet's wives covered in front of a blind man. We will return to this broader meaning of the *hijab* at the end of this chapter.

Who is morally responsible for maintaining *hijab*, and thus preventing illicit interactions, is also not entirely clear. Verse 33:53 can be understood to address primarily men, not women. This interpretation is supported in hadith, such as the one cited earlier that was relayed by the Prophet's servant Anas Ibn Malik. In this tradition, the *hijab* is instigated by men (lingering wedding guests), drawn by a man (the Prophet), in order to immediately separate two men (the Prophet and his servant).

Nevertheless, most Qur'anic commentators assume this verse presents a vision of proper gender relations, with specific directives aimed at women. For example, many argue that 33:53 establishes a principle of seclusion of the Prophet's wives, who had until that time participated fully in the public affairs of the Muslim community. This raises a further challenge, mainly of the exact relationship of the Prophet's wives to the moral lives of common believers. On one hand, these women are held up as moral exemplars in the Qur'an. On the other hand, the Qur'an itself tells us they are not similar to other women (33:32), implying they cannot be perfectly emulated. We also have hadith reports that assume *hijab* is the very thing that distinguishes the Prophet's wives from other Muslim women. According to the tradition in Muhammad Bukhari's (d. 870) collection, for instance, the Prophet's companions were at first unsure if the Prophet planned to marry Safiya or just keep her as a slave. They decided 'if he covers/secludes her [*in hajaba-ha*], she is one of the Mothers of the Believers, but if he doesn't cover/seclude her [*lan yahjub-ha*], she is one of his slaves'. When the Prophet mounted his horse with Safiya behind him, 'he spread a *hijab* between her and the people', and thus his companions knew he would marry her (Bukhari 1976–9, vol. 6, 121). In this way, *hijab* was also a sign of privilege in the early Muslim community.

Verse 33:53, despite being known as the 'verse of the veil', does not entail a clear mandate for all Muslim women to cover. Human attempts to interpret this verse are complicated by three factors. There are multiple meanings of *hijab* in the Qur'an, none of which have anything to do with a woman's dress. The normative assumptions of this verse are unclear, including whether or not it is primarily interested in gender relations, or protection of the Prophet's privacy. Finally, even if we agree this verse is about the seclusion of the Prophet's wives, it is unclear how to apply this example to the lives of common believers. Given their elite status, the 'mothers of the believers' had heightened moral responsibilities. An ongoing debate among Islamic scholars, especially feminist ones, is how do Muslim women follow the example of the Prophet's wives who were extraordinary?

Verse 33:59: protection outside the home

According to hadith, verse 33:59 follows soon after the '*hijab* verse', and has been linked by Qur'anic interpreters to the issue of veiling. Sometimes called the 'mantle verse', it reads as follows:

> O Prophet, say to thy wives and daughters and the believing women, that they draw their veils [*jalibab*, sing. *jilbab*] close to them; so it is likelier they will be known, and not hurt. God is All-forgiving, All-compassionate (Arberry 1996, vol. 2, 128).

> O Prophet! Tell your wives and daughters, and the believing women, that they should cast their outer garments [*jalibab*, sing. *jilbab*] over their persons (when abroad): that is most convenient, that they should be known (as such) and not molested. And God is Oft-Forgiving, Most Merciful (Ali 2010, 320).

In this revelation, all Muslim women are encouraged to draw close their *jilbab,* so that they will be recognized, and not harassed or molested. From a tradition recorded by Ibn Sa'ad, we know the following about the occasion of this revelation:

> When the wives of the Prophet of Allah, Allah bless him and grant him salvation, had gone out at night by necessity, some of the hypocrites used to prevent them and molest them. They [the people] complained about it. But the hypocrites said, 'We do it

to the slave-girls only'. Then this Qur'anic verse [33:59] was revealed.

This hadith report describes the public harassment of women in Medina as so common that any woman who went out at night to relieve herself risked attack. The 'hypocrites' referred to here are Muslim trouble-makers or 'agitators' (33:60), who engage in activities they know to be immoral. This hadith report blames 'hypocrites' for the public assaults on women, although it is also important to stress that in that specific cultural context, slave women were understood to be available to free men for sex. Even if a wide range of what we would today call 'sexual harassment' occurred in Medina in this period, verse 33:59 is concerned only with protecting free Muslim women from attacks. *Jilbab* was the primarily way to visually mark someone as a free woman and therefore not sexually available in the same way as a slave.

The understanding of this specific context (harassment of women on the streets of Medina) and purpose (to prevent harassment of free Muslim women) remained mostly consistent in Qur'anic commentary from the ninth to fifteenth centuries, even as the definition of what *jilbab* was, and what parts of a woman's body it covered, changed. The challenge is that there is no way to know for sure what seventh-century *jilbab* looked like. Arberry translates it as 'veil'; Ali as 'outer garment'. Other common translations include 'mantle' and 'cloak'. Most scholars believe it was some sort of total body covering.

With the addition of verse 33:59, the story of 'what the Qur'an says about veiling' is further complicated. In contrast to *hijab*, at least interpreters agree that *jilbab* refers to an article of women's clothing. In contrast to 33:53, verse 33:59 is concerned with all Muslim women, not just the prophet's wives. It is a woman's responsibility to draw her outer garments around her, even if this self-protection is necessitated because of the immoral behavior of some men. This verse is also more explicitly concerned with inappropriate sexual relations between men and women than 33:53. Finally, the focus in 33:59 is on female appearance outside the home, not their privacy or seclusion within. However, as some contemporary scholars have argued, it is not clear how the need to cover in order 'to be known as free' translates into a contemporary society that has abolished slavery, and does not approve of the public harassment of any woman (Wadud 1999).

Verse 24:30–31: sexual modesty

The third piece of Qur'anic evidence often quoted in support of veiling is verse 24:30–31. We have very few reports in the canonical hadith collections providing us with the context for this revelation, and those we do have appeared later, in the fourteenth and fifteenth centuries, when veiling practices had already been established in Muslim communities. Complicating things further, the specific Arabic terms used in the verse have various and contentious meanings.

The verse reads as follows:

Say to the believers, that they cast down their eyes and guard their private parts [*furujahun*]; that is purer for them. God is aware of the things they work. And say to the believing women, that they cast down their eyes and guard their private parts, and reveal not their adornment [*zina*] save such as is outward; and let them cast their veils [*khumur*, sing. *khimar*] over their bosoms [*juyub*], and not reveal their adornment [*zina*] save to their husbands, or their fathers, or their husband's fathers, or their sons, or their husbands' sons, or their brothers, or their brothers' sons, or their sister's sons, or their women, or what their right hands own, or such men as attend them, not having sexual desire, or children who have not yet attained knowledge of women's private parts [*'awra*]; not let them stamp their feet, so that their hidden ornament may be known. And turn all together to God, O you believers; haply so you will prosper (Arberry 1996, vol. 2, 49–50).

Say to the believing men that they should lower their gaze and guard their modesty [*furujahun*]: that will make for greater purity for them: and God is well acquainted with all that they do. And say to the believing women that they should lower their gaze and guard their modesty; that they should not display their beauty and ornaments [*zina*] except what (must ordinarily) appear thereof; that they should draw their veils [*khumur*, sing. *khimar*] over their bosoms [*juyub*] and not display their beauty [*zina*] except to their husbands, their fathers, their husband's fathers, their sons, their husbands' sons, their brothers or their brother's sons, or their sister's sons, or their women, or the slaves whom their right hands possess, or male servants free of physical needs, or small children who have no sense of the shame of sex [*'awra*]; and that they should not strike their feet in order to draw attention to their hidden ornaments. And O you Believers! You turn all together toward God, that you may attain Bliss (Ali 2010, 261–262).

Here women are directed not to reveal some sort of hidden *zina* and to cover their *'awra* in front of men except close male relatives or male servants. Unfortunately, the meanings of both *zina* and *'awra* are unclear in this text.

Zina has a specific meaning in Islamic law of illicit sex (see chapter 3), however it has a much more general meaning the 43 times it occurs in the Qur'an. At times it refers to people (10:24 and 13:33), but it also describes the beauty of the stars (37:6), heaven (41:12), and sky (50:6). This means in general terms the Qur'anic meaning of *zina* is morally neutral: it is merely a state of attractiveness.

Throughout history, Qur'anic commentators have disagreed over what makes up the category of hidden *zina* in verse 24:31, and thus what must be covered. We have one hint in the verse itself: the directive 'not strike their feet in order to draw attention to their hidden ornaments' suggests that noise-making anklets might be an example of adornment that should be hidden.

Specific women and body parts are exempt from covering. Verse (24:60), for instance, frees elderly women from the charge to conceal their adornments. Al-Tabari (d. 932), one of the earliest interpreters of the Qur'an, allows faces and hands to show, even faces with makeup and ringed fingers, but includes bracelets, anklets, and necklaces as hidden adornment that should be covered (Hoffman 1998, 92). He bases his interpretation on a hadith report in which the Prophet explains that the face and hands of a woman who has reached the age of menarche are exempt from the directive to cover: '"When a woman starts menstruating, she is not allowed to show [her body] except for her face and within this extent," then he grabbed his own arm, leaving the part between wrist and palm' (al-Tabari vol. 18, 93 translated by Goto 2004, 288). For al-Zamakhshari (d. 1144), *zina* refers only to things a woman puts on, such as jewelry or makeup. He argues that a woman's face and hands may always show because 'to cover them causes difficulty, for the woman has no recourse but to work with her hands, and she must show her face, especially to give testimony and to appear in court and to marry, and she must walk in the streets showing her feet, especially if she is poor' (translated in Hoffman 1998, 92, 116n21).

On the strictest end of the spectrum are Islamic scholars who want all of a woman's natural beauty to be covered. Ibn Taymiyya (d. 1328) and al-Baydawi (d. 1282), for instance, allow women's faces and hands to be uncovered only during prayer (Hoffman 1998, 94).

Soraya Hajjaji-Jarrah makes a compelling argument about the meaning of hidden *zina* in 24:31 based on a commonality she identifies in the Qur'anic useage of *zina*: it always refers to enhancing some aspect that is inessential or extraneous to the person or thing. For Hajjaji-Jarrah this implies that hidden *zina* cannot refer to the attractiveness of a woman's hair, face, arms, or legs, as 'these parts of the female body are neither unessential, nor extraneous, nor fundamentally intended to enhance the appearance of a woman … they are essential parts of the human anatomy' (Hajjaji-Jarrah 2003, 188).

'*Awra* has its own interpretative complexity. Arberry translates it as 'women's private parts'; Ali translates it as 'shame of sex'. Verse 24:30–31 specifies several categories of males for whom women's hidden '*awra* need not be covered at all, mainly her close male relatives (her father, father-in-law, son, step-son, brother, nephew), male servants (both slaves and eunuchs), and young boys. In these cases it is assumed exposure of a woman's '*awra* will not create illicit sexual desires. This all implies that '*awra* is tied to women's sexual genitalia. In verse 24:30, however, the word *furujahan* is used to refer to the genitalia of men, which raises the question of why 24:31 uses a different word to refer to women's genitals?

A semantic use of '*awra* not limited to bodies emerges if we consider its meaning in the other two verses it is found in the Qur'an. '*Awra* is used in 33:13 to describe defenseless homes, and in 24:58 '*awra* refers to the times of the day when interruption by servants or children is likely. A fairer translation of the Qur'anic use of '*awra* would thus be 'a vulnerable thing'.

Since in verse 24:31 '*awra* refers to an actual part of a woman's body, we still need to determine what part of the body in this verse is deemed 'vulnerable'. Both commentators on the Qur'an and Islamic jurists (see chapter 3) have defined '*awra* in various ways for both men and women. In general, '*awra* for men is the area between the navel and the knees and the majority of hadith

reports addressing covering *'awra* are directed at men, which suggests that it was men, not women, who tended to violate modesty norms in the early Muslim community. And although often
neglected in contemporary discussions of veiling, head covering
of men was also common in the early Muslim community. Hadith
reports mention Muhammad wearing a turban and occasionally
covering his face as a sign of respect for his elders (Abu Dawud
and Bukhari translated by El Guindi 1999, 106, 119).

There is no scholarly consensus about the definition of a
woman's *'awra*. This is not helped by the fact that the hadith rarely
discuss *'awra* and women. The one isolated but influential exception is a hadith recorded by Tirmidhi which implies women's
entire bodies are *'awra*: 'Woman is *'awra*. If she goes out, Satan
attempts to control her' (translated in Clarke 2003, 218). This
hadith is the basis for some Islamic scholars' belief that women
should cover entirely, from head to toe. In some legal opinions,
even a woman's voice is found to be *'awra* (El Fadl 2001, 185).
But for other scholars, a woman's *'awra* does not include her
hands and face; for others it is only her bosom, neck and head;
and for still others, as with men, it refers only to her genitals.

Since the meanings of both *zina* and *'awra* are up for debate,
it is not particularly helpful that in verse 24:30–31 the things a
woman must cover are defined by these terms. Luckily, we are
given a few other hints in the verse itself. For one, we are told
some specific actions that are required to cover *zina* and *'awra*,
including the covering of *juyub* with *khimar*. The root of *juyub*
means an *opening* or *space between*. Although it is often translated
as bosom, it is technically a woman's cleavage. *Khimar*, a term
some commentators gloss as veil, refers to a specific type of
clothing, mainly a kerchief. In other words, the verse tells us that
cleavage is part of hidden *'awra* and thus should be covered by
something a woman wears.

In contrast, a phrase that comes earlier in the verse asks
women to 'lower their gaze' and thus ties modesty not to what a

woman wears or conceals, but to her actions. Qur'anic commentators have tended to interpret averting the eyes metaphorically as avoiding desiring what is forbidden. Elsewhere in the Qur'an (e.g. 33:33) modesty is juxtaposed against *tabarruj*, an overt form of flirtation that involves prancing, flaunting, and embellishing with the goal of attracting attention. As al-Tabari states in his commentary on 24:31 'looking corrupts the heart' (translated in Hoffman 1998, 92, 116n15). This expands modesty beyond dress to include a virtuous demeanor.

Verse 24:30–31 is difficult to interpret, which is not helped by the absence of any solid hadith concerning the occasion of its revelation. The text directs both men and women to be modest, however it devotes substantially more time to discussing women's modesty. Specific actions are required for women (such as covering bosoms and *'awra*) and others are forbidden (such as drawing attention to themselves). Verse 24:30–31 also conceives women's beauty as a particular obstacle to realizing modesty norms. Unlike the earlier veiling revelations, it explicitly references women's modesty, an article of clothing that is sometimes used to cover a head (even if no reference to the head or hair is made), and is directed towards all Muslim women. While verse 33:59 referred to sexual assault, and thus the problematic sexual appetite of men, in verse 24:30–31 we see the focus shifted to how women's bodies create this inappropriate sexual desire in the first place. Finally, in verse 24:30–31, modesty is conveyed through social interaction in ways that go beyond dress.

Summary

At the close of this chapter, the reader probably still has more questions than answers about what Islamic sacred texts say about the veil. The Qur'an and hadith simply do not give a definitive answer to some of the most basic questions about the veil.

Sacred texts, because they require human interpretation of divine revelation, turn out to be a source of confusion, not clarity.

The three relevant Qur'anic verses contain tremendous diversity, especially in regards to what the veil is, who has a duty to veil, and for what reason. Three different Arabic words are used in the Qur'an that might be translated as the Islamic veil: *hijab*, *jilbab*, *khimar*. *Jilbab* and *khimar* at least refer to articles of clothing, but not the same ones. A cloak covers the body; a kerchief usually covers a head, and in 24:31 it specifically covers a woman's cleavage. The common Qur'anic meaning of *hijab* is not clothing at all, but rather a separation, and in 33:53 *hijab* seems to refer to a physical screen. All three terms can be interpreted as gender barriers, but they separate men and women in different ways (hiding, making recognizable, covering) for different norms (privacy, bodily integrity, modesty).

The three verses address different groups of women for whom the veil is recommended. In verse 33:53, only the Prophet's wives are addressed. In 33:59, the veil is recommended for free Muslim women. In verse 24:31, all Muslim women are told to lower their gaze and cover their hidden *zina* and *'awra*. To complicate things further, men are also discussed in the sacred texts, both as the reason why the *hijab* is drawn, as well as having their own duty to be modest. In fact, the hadith as a whole is more concerned with the modest dress of men than women, especially with regards to prayer and during hajj when special ritualized clothing is prescribed.

Another difference between the three verses is why a separation of men and women is required in the first place and thus the moral norm the separation supports. In verse 33:53, the veil safeguards the *privacy* of the Prophet's home life. Here seclusion ensures that the Prophet's wives are not bothered in their home through creating a separation of public and private spaces. The concern is with the protection of *bodily integrity* of Muslim women, in verse 33:59. The veil here protects women from unjust sexual harassment and assault when they are outside their homes. Finally, verse 24:31 establishes guidelines for interactions between men and women in order to encourage *modesty* and prevent inappropriate sexual relations.

Note that fundamental to understanding these sacred texts on the issue of the veil is the initial interpretative move that these verses are intimately related. In fact, a Qur'anic 'Islamic veil' is only possible through a holistic reading of the Qur'an that links these verses and semantically expands the meaning of each. In other words, only by interpolating the revelation recorded in 33:59 about harassment of women and cloaks, the revelation in verse 24:31 about sexual modesty and kerchiefs, and verse 33:53 about the Prophet's privacy and a curtain, is the concept of *an* 'Islamic veil' sensible. Only by linking the key terms (*hijab*, *jilbab*, *khimar*) and norms (privacy, bodily integrity, modesty) can a scriptural basis for an Islamic veil that applies to all women be seen.

This process of interpolation is inclusive and additive insofar as the most expansive meanings are incorporated. This is how the seclusion of 33:53 comes to be understood by some to apply to all Muslim women: it is logically combined with 24:31, which does address all believers. This is also how wearing the cloak of 33:59 is considered to be a duty of modesty: it is linked to the norm of modesty in 24:31 and thereby extends what should be covered beyond cleavage. And this is also how the *hijab* in 33:53 becomes an article of clothing women wear outside the home.

The fundamental interpretive move of linking these three verses was already taking place in the hadith. For instance, in a report of the infamous incident in which one of the Prophet's favored wives, 'A'isha, was left behind by a caravan and then rescued by a handsome young man, 'A'isha recounts that the man recognized her because 'he used to see me before the *hijab*' and she 'drew her *jilbab* around her', since it was 'after the *hijab* came down' (Bukhari translated by Clarke 2003, 233). Other hadith reports reference a time 'after the hijab came down'. This means by the time hadith was recorded, *hijab* had already been transformed from a literal thing (curtain) to a complex ideology of gender segregation, privacy, and social status. And since hadith were recorded after the Prophet's death, this expanded meaning of the *hijab* may reflect cultural practices of specific Muslim communities rather than an accurate interpretation of revelation.

3
Law

Islamic law is often blamed for the oppression of Muslims, especially Muslim women. Non-Muslims and Muslims alike are under the impression that there is one, homogenous legal code that spells out the rules for Muslims' lives. This misunderstanding is based on part on the tendency to collapse two concepts related to Islamic law: shari'a and *fiqh*. Shari'a is an Arabic word whose original meaning was 'path to the water hole'; in the Qur'an, shari'a refers to the clear and right path that believers should follow (45:18). Today the term is used by Muslims to refer to the complete, infallible, universal law of God. Because human beings are imperfect and fallible, shari'a cannot be entirely known or implemented. *Fiqh*, in contrast, is the system of rules for Muslims that jurists develop in their ongoing attempt to understand and implement shari'a. This means there are two key conceptual distinctions: 1) between shari'a and *fiqh* as respectively perfect and divine versus human and imperfect and 2) between theory and application, where the shari'a is a set of abstract principles, and *fiqh* is the application of those principles to specific historical and social contexts. To make things more complicated, drawing one distinction does not necessarily require one to draw the other. Some conservative Muslims, for example, might agree that *fiqh* is diverse and context-specific (whereas shari'a is not), yet do not believe it is necessary fallible. This conceptual diversity is one reason why opinions about what 'Islamic law' says about veiling differ greatly.

Legal reasoning has had enormous influence on the development of Muslim meanings for the veil. Islamic legal scholars work to elaborate, apply, and explain the meaning of the veil as described in sacred texts, and Islamic legal thought is referenced in contemporary efforts to establish national legislation requiring the veil. This chapter will not survey all the legal opinions (*fiqh*) on the Islamic veil, nor declare what Islamic law 'really says' about the veil. The first task is made difficult, if not impossible, by the long and varied history of Islamic legal thought and the enormous body of texts this endeavor produced. The second task is not possible because diversity is part of the system of legal reasoning in Islam. Instead, this chapter focuses on three tasks: introducing the texts, institutions, sources, and modes of reasoning in classical Islamic legal thought; explaining the manner in which medieval jurists interpret *'awra* (vulnerable thing) within the logic of *fitna* (disorder) and its impact on the veil; and describing modern attempts to legislate compulsory veiling. These three sections will help the reader to understand the nature of Islamic legal thought and its effect on contemporary discourses about the veil.

Classical Islamic legal interpretation: institutions, sources, and texts

When the Prophet Muhammad was alive, he could provide direct ethical guidance to Muslims, by receiving and interpreting revelation directly from God, as well as providing a model for right action. Upon his death, moral authority became more complicated and a major break between Sunni and Shi'a arose from competing claims about who should provide leadership after the death of the Prophet Muhammad. Sunnis recognize the caliphs, beginning with Muhammad's companion Abu Bakr, as the legitimate successors of the Prophet Muhammad. For Sunnis, the first four caliphs (known as the 'the rightly guided' or *rashidun*) acted as legal guides for the community.

But for Shiʻa, legitimate religious guidance was much different after the death of the prophet. Shiʻa recognize the Imams, beginning with Muhammad's companion and son-in-law Ali, as the rightful successors to the Prophet. Imams had a legal function similar to the Prophet in that they are designated by God, directly instructed believers, and were infallible. Imams did not, however, receive new revelation directly. Instead, they served as reliable interpreters of duties and rights described in the Qurʼan, and exemplified by the Prophet's actions. For Twelver Shiʻa (Shiʻa who believe in twelve Imams), when the last Imam 'went into hiding' in the ninth century and the Age of Occultation began, reliable legal guidance became more complicated, as discussed later in the section on Iran. Regardless of this schism, Shiʻas remained the minority in most regions (important exceptions include Iran, Iraq, and Lebanon). Particularly during the early history of the Muslim community, Sunni understandings of authority had the widest influence on the development of legal thinking and institutions.

During the Umayyad dynasty (661–750, the second of the four major Arab caliphates established after the death of Muhammad), Islam expanded in terms of geography and influence, and the application of legal guidance shifted to appointed judges (*qadis*). These judges were dispatched throughout the dynasty to apply *fiqh* when various complaints were registered with the court. This meant that they based their rulings on customary laws in the area they were stationed and personal interpretations of the Qurʼan. They made decisions about legal matters somewhat independently, and the result was a system of contradictory and unpredictable decisions.

In the ninth century, legal schools (*madhhab*, pl. *madhahib*) worked hard to reform this ad hoc system of interpreting Islamic law. Four main Sunni and a number of Shiʻi legal schools formed around influential legal thinkers for whom they were named: Hanbali, Hanafi, Maliki, Shafi'i, and Jafari. While these schools came to emphasize different sources of law, they operated with a level of mutual respect. In terms of the Islamic veil, different opinions existed within the same school and jurists in different schools shared opinions.

Each school of law attempted to improve the interpretation of shari'a by suggesting a methodology (*usul al-fiqh*) or 'a coherent system of principles through which a qualified jurist could extract rulings for novel cases' (Hallaq 1984, 5). Part of this method was determining appropriate sources for legal thinking. All the *madhahib* recognized the Qur'an as the first source of Islamic law. As discussed in chapter 2, it is a source revealed directly by God and thus has binding legal authority. The second source of consensus was the Sunna of the Prophet, as recorded in the hadith. Since the Prophet was the only infallible interpreter of the Qur'an, hadith are particularly important for clarifying legal principles of the Qur'an.

While the Qur'an and hadith reports do provide guidelines for right living, they are not exhaustive. This meant early jurists had to consider other avenues to reach decisions in cases not explicitly addressed by the Qur'an or the hadith. One such avenue was through consultation of *ijma'*, or consensus. *Ijma'* was considered a reliable source of guidance based on the Prophet's saying, 'My community will never agree in error'. The prominence of *ijma'* in Islamic legal reasoning helps to explain why opinions about veiling often reflected cultural practices common in the jurist's community. Finally, jurists relied on *qiyas*, or analogy, to deduce legal rules from similar rules in the Qur'an or hadith.

The idea of a codified, self-contained, singular version of 'Islamic law' is a modern and Western one, supported by European orientalists in the late nineteenth and early twentieth centuries who envisioned a 'Muslim world' with a particularly stubborn form of canon law (Khalafallah 2005, 38). In truth, classical

Islamic legal thought has always entailed a process of readjustment and application not only of the rules, but also mechanisms for applying the message of Islam to specific real life challenges facing Muslims. Although there was no single canon, legal scholars produced and consulted a variety of textual sources to assist them with their endeavors such as manuals of legal schools (*mutun*), legal commentaries (*shuruh*), and non-binding legal opinions (*fatwas*) on a specific issue. Crucial to understanding Islamic legal texts is the manner in which texts accept different and evolving interpretations of Islamic law. For example, while there has not been much change in the manuals since the ninth century, *shuruh* and *fatwas* continued to be produced and reflect an ever-increasing diversity of legal thought. Not only did schools easily house more than one opinion on a given issue, contradictory opinions in the same texts, or even authored by the same jurist, were the norm (Khalafallah 2005, 49).

One final note. Feminist scholars have pointed out the danger in privileging *fiqh* as a source of guidelines for veiling. For one, men authored most legal texts. This is not to say that women were uninvolved in the formation and practice of Islamic law. For instance, women were active in shari'a courts: they brought cases, advocated for their rights, registered business transactions, and sued former husbands. But men were the producers of written *fiqh*, which therefore may reflect male biases about women in general and veiling in particular. Second, most *fiqh* assumes gender complementarity and therefore that men and women have different rights and duties. That the issue of modesty was not discussed in the same way in reference to men and women reflects a trend in much legal reasoning to consider women's bodies as in more need of regulation.

Looking at its formative period shows us a number of important things about Islamic law. First, Islamic law does not entail a single universal law or code for specific actions, such as veiling. It is best understood as an ongoing process in which Muslim legal thinkers explain and justify their opinions and issues are rarely definitively resolved. Second, while the ninth-century legal schools worked to systematize patterns of legal reasoning through recognizing *ijma'* and *qiyas* as sources of shari'a, they continued to accept diverse opinions in different Muslim communities. This diversity is reflected in the history of jurisprudence, which makes room for minority opinions. This is important to keep in mind: despite our interest in figuring out what Islamic law says about the veil, we need to realize the answer is always multiple. Finally, the development of legal thought did not occur in a vacuum. As legal scholar Kecia Ali has argued, everyone is influenced by their own social, cultural, and religious backgrounds and 'the early jurists were no exception to this rule; like contemporary Muslim thinkers, they could not help but be influenced by their own sense of what was right and wrong, natural and unnatural' (Ali 2006, xxvi). Ali's insight encourages us to be mindful and even suspicious of the cultural contexts in which opinions were issued and how these might differ from those of the present.

Medieval legal concerns: faces and *fitna*

Early *fiqh* discussed veiling in the context of prayer, and in general saw veiling as an issue of social status and physical safety (El Fadl 2001, 233, 255–256n106). This changed in medieval *fiqh*. Although women's dress was not a central concern of medieval legal scholars, themes and concepts that emerged in legal reasoning during this time period remain relevant in modern discussions of the veil.

One interesting trend in medieval legal reasoning was an increase in discussions about the interpretation of *'awra* and whether or not a woman should cover her face. In chapter 2 we saw that face-veiling was not mentioned in the Qur'anic revelation. Hadith reports also tell us it was not a common practice within the early Muslim community. However in medieval legal reasoning, face-veiling gained some prominence. There was by no means a legal consensus, but a majority legal opinion (women should cover everything expect face and hands) and a minority opinion (women should cover everything except the eyes) emerged. It was Ibn Taymiyyah's (d. 1328) opinion, for example, that women should cover their faces in public, and this became the standard Hanbali and Shafi'i position. In contrast, the Hanafi scholar Burhan al-Din al-Marghinani (d. 1197) wrote about the importance of women's faces and hands remaining uncovered, especially during everyday business transactions with men. For the most part, Maliki and Hanafi legal experts did not consider a woman's face or hands part of *'awra*. But even these standard legal positions were within specific schools were not universal.

Another common pattern of legal reasoning in medieval *fiqh* is the linkage of *'awra* (vulnerability) and *fitna*. Specifically, it was during this time that jurists began to rely on a doctrine of *fitna*, or worldly disorder, to justify rulings on a wide range of issues (El Fadl 2001, 233). The word *fitna* appears in a number of places in the Qur'an where it refers to non-sexual temptations, such as money, that lead to discord or worldly disorder. It is not, however, used in the sacred text as a reason for veiling, nor even to refer to actions and things that produce sexual arousal and lead to sexual sin. However, the majority of medieval legal scholars utilized a doctrine of *fitna* to explain why the covering of women was required. The disorder at stake was the chaos that sexual desire outside of marriage can cause (such as distraction from completing other duties). The basic idea was that, while Islam affirms sexuality as a human good, sexual desire nonetheless is so powerful that it can lead men and women to have inappropriate sexual encounters. The following opinion by jurist al-Nawawi (d. 1278) is exemplary of this legal reasoning:

> Since God made men desire women, and desire looking at them, and enjoying them, women are like the devil in that they seduce men towards the commission of evil, while making evil look attractive [to men]. We deduct from this that women should not go out in the midst of men except for a necessity (translated in El Fadl 2001, 237).

When applied to the veil, this doctrine cast veiling as a broader sociological concern related to regulating boundaries between men and women. Centuries later, this same concern motivates the arguments of some emerging Islamic governments, who claim that their stability depends on the public veiling of all women.

Historian Judith Tucker identifies three zones of male-female interaction assumed in *fiqh* (Tucker 2008, 183–184). One zone is the marital zone in which sexual desire is not only lawful, but is encouraged and necessary. A second zone is neutral in terms of sexual desire and here there is no fear of *fitna*. This zone is where interactions with relatives, young girls, or elderly women occur. For example, Ibn Taymiyya (d. 1328) argued that women do not need to cover in front of male servants without sexual desire such as eunuchs. As al-Qurtubi (d. 1273) bluntly stated, 'If the woman is beautiful and if there is fear of *fitna* from her face and hands, her duty is to cover them. And if she is old and ugly, she is allowed to uncover her face and hands' (al-Qurtubi translated by Goto 2004, 291). The zone that jurists are concerned with is a third zone of illicit desire between unmarried adults where *fitna* might occur. This zone is legally regulated in order to minimize sexual appeal and interaction. While medieval legal scholars saw male sexual impulse as the primary force to be controlled, they understood female beauty to be the primary cause of this impulse. Their regulations were therefore directed to women's bodies.

The Muslim jurist Khaled Abou El Fadl (b. 1963) points out a number of logical problems with making fear of *fitna* the reason why women have a duty to veil in public. For one, this makes veiling's primary goal the avoidance of *fitna*, thus neglecting its other shari'a values. ''*Awra* and *fitna* are separate categories – a person covers the '*awra* not because of *fitna*, but because the covering of '*awra* is a separate imperative based on a set of specific instructions. Whether revealing the '*awra* leads or does not lead to *fitna* is irrelevant' (El Fadl 2001, 235). According to El Fadl, modesty is an ethical command in and of itself in the Qur'an, independent of whether it causes *fitna*.

Second, relying on a doctrine of *fitna* to make the Islamic veil obligatory for women shifts the blame for the potential sin from men to women. In the previous chapter's discussion of the Qur'an, we saw that the hypocrites were blamed for violations of modesty (33:59–60), and the *hijab* was drawn because of loitering male guests (33:53). Medieval jurists, in contrast, focused on regulating women's bodies as instigators of *fitna*. El Fadl suggests 'demanding that women should suffer exclusion or limitations would violate the principle that the innocent should not pay for the indiscretions of the culpable' (El Fadl 2001, 234–235).

Third, even jurists who had very expansive interpretations of what women had to cover to avoid *fitna* allowed for exceptions based on what would ordinarily be shown as part of custom (*'adah*), nature (*jibillah*), and necessity (*darurah*). Slaves who labored in fields, for example, did not have a legal obligation to cover their arms because their normal economic activity required physical mobility. El Fadl argues that this sort of exemption 'means that the rules of veiling are contingent and contextual in nature' (El Fadl 2001, 241).

When medieval legal experts discussed '*awra* or *fitna*, their main focus was not on veiling per se, but the prevention and punishment of illicit sexual encounters. Nevertheless, they linked *fitna* to the veil thereby by marking women's bodies as dangerous and disorderly. At the same time, their reliance on local veiling practices to determine what constitutes *'awra* continued the legal precedent for multiple and varied interpretations of what the veil should cover and what it physically looked like.

Twentieth-century codification of modern Islamic legal codes

The late nineteenth and early twentieth century marked a significant turning point in Islamic legal thought on the veil. For one, there was a new juridical interest in the veil that accompanied modernization reforms targeting women. Jurists began to address both the covering and uncovering of women within the context of programs aimed at changing women's access to education, roles in child-rearing, and participation in public life. As Judith Tucker argues, 'these debates were legal debates, strictly speaking, only in small part; rather, they were wide-ranging discussions focused on the sociological challenges mounted by the demands of modernity to Islam and local custom' (Tucker 2008, 200).

This increased interest sparked a wide range of legal opinions about whether women should veil or unveil, even within the same country. For example, in the midst of national debate over modernization in Egypt, discussed in chapter 4, the jurist Qasim Amin (d. 1908) came out strongly against face-veiling. However, Muhammad 'Abduh (d. 1905), the Grand Mufti in Egypt at the time, declined to give an opinion. The opinion of jurist Rashid Rida (d. 1935) was that the veil should be used but women should not be secluded, based on the fact that women in early Islam were active in public life. The Fatwa Committee of Al-Azhar in Cairo delayed giving a decision until 1937, when it merely summarized the Hanafi position, which was not opposed to unveiling, and the Maliki one, which maintained veiling was not a religious requirement. In Tunisia, al-Tahir al-Haddad (d. 1935) argued against the face-veil on the grounds that it did not create modesty, but rather tried physically to restrain immodesty, much like 'putting a muzzle on a dog's mouth to prevent bites' (translated by Tucker 2008, 201). However, this was only one among many legal opinions in Tunisia: other local Hanafi and Maliki jurists maintained that the veiling of all but the eyes was required because of widespread immorality (Tucker 2008, 202).

Second, there were attempts in this time period to make Islamic law more 'modern' by writing fixed codes of 'shari'a law'. As a part of this process, many legal systems in Muslim majority countries developed Islamic personal status and family codes. This meant that laws that affected women, such as those pertaining to divorce, inheritance, and custody, became based on a particular nineteenth-century interpretation of the shari'a. By the 1920s, Islamic personal status laws existed in Algeria, Egypt, Indonesia, Iran, Iraq, Jordan, Kuwait, Lebanon, Libya, Morocco, Pakistan, Sudan, Syria, Tunisia, and Yemen. These personal status laws proved resilient. For example, the *Tanzimat* (1839) legal reforms of the Ottoman Empire left Islamic family law untouched despite reforming almost every aspect of Turkish law.

Most of these Islamic personal status laws, however, did not address veiling. But this new trend of codifying law changed the way Muslims understood religious legal guidance and set the stage for more extensive codifications of Islamic law, some of which affected the legal status of the veil. For one, the effort to codify changed Islamic law from a fluid, ad hoc system of texts and opinions to a legal system with a written, predictable canon law. In addition, the nature of shari'a authority changed with codification. Islamic courts, such as the courts in the

Ottoman Empire, functioned with various levels of autonomy from political leaders. That changed in the nineteenth century when nation-states began to write Islamic legal codes backed by the authority of the state. Finally, the purpose of law changed in this period. Islamic law became something that the state could use to regulate populations. In some areas, especially Iran and Pakistan, Islamic legal codes helped legitimate new Islamic forms of government. By establishing easily identifiable 'Islamic laws' these states displayed cultural legitimacy and were able to draw on Islamic authority to police the population. Shari'a thus became the basis for state punitive power (Ali 2010, 4–5).

Based on the legal opinion that the covering of Muslim women should be compulsory, there are a number of countries that currently regulate the veiling of women. Sudan's criminal code allows the flogging or fining of anyone who 'violates public morality or wears indecent clothing'. In Pakistan government employees are required to veil. In Indonesia and Tajikistan veiling requirements have recently been imposed on some schoolgirls. This section will focus on three situations in which public veiling became mandatory for all women: post-revolutionary Iran since 1979, Saudi Arabia since the establishment of its Islamic monarchy in 1932, and Taliban rule of Afghanistan, from 1996 to 2001.

Post-revolutionary Iran

A mass wardrobe change takes place on board every international flight into Tehran. Once the pilot announces the plane has begun its initial descent, every woman not already veiled pulls some form of Islamic dress from her carry-on and quickly covers her head in order to be in compliance with Iranian law. In contemporary Iran, by national legal decree, every woman must wear Islamic dress (locally referred to as *hijab*) including a head covering.

Iran's Assembly of Experts met in 1979, after a revolution removed the monarchy from power and established an Islamic government. Their first task was to write a new constitution based on the Qur'an. The resulting constitution declares that all 'civil, penal, financial, economic, administrative, cultural, military, political, and other laws and regulations [in Iran] must be based on Islamic criteria' (Art. 4). Although veiling was not initially mandatory, a 1983 amendment to the constitution made it illegal for a woman to appear in public without Islamic dress. Article 638 of the Iranian Penal Code, ratified in 1996, lays out punishment for improper veiling as seventy-four lashes, jail sentence of up to two months, or a fine of 500,000 rials (approximately 55 USD or 40 Euros).

Since Ayatollah Ruhollah Khomeini (d. 1989) is often credited – or blamed – by both Iranians and outsiders for the status of the Islamic veil in Iran, a look at his opinion on the veil is warranted. Take, for example, the following legal opinion, expressed informally during a 1978 interview before the Revolution: 'In Islam women must dress modestly and wear a veil, but that does not necessarily mean she has to wear chador. Women can choose any kind of attire they like so long as it covers them properly and they have *hijab*' (Khomeini 2001, 85–86). Here the duty to publicly cover is confirmed by Khomeini, even as the definition of a proper Islamic veil is never specified.

What becomes significant in the Iranian context is that this same ambiguity gets codified in national laws and local regulations, all of which require the use of an Islamic veil in public, but fail to explicitly define it. For example, the Penal Code states that a woman must wear 'shari'a defined *hijab*'. But as we have seen, legal experts disagree about what the shari'a says about *hijab*. Even in Iran, each jurist has an opinion about women's dress: some are concerned with ankles, others with gold rings, still others with make-up or bouffant hair. This diversity is reflected in their respective definitions of proper Islamic dress: one jurist will require socks, another specify colors for *manteaus* (coat-like garments), yet another will prohibit certain images on clothing (like a wolf) as too masculine or aggressive, or even ban sequins or shoes that make noise when a woman walks. This creates a legal context which both requires public veiling and allows each woman to choose what form of veil she wears.

Saudi Arabia and the Basic Law

In the eighteenth century, Muhammad ibn Abd al-Wahhab (d. 1792), leader of the ultraconservative Islamic Wahhabi movement, and Muhammad ibn Saud (d. 1765), head of the royal Saudi family (House of Saud), formed an allegiance of faith and politics. This laid the groundwork for the modern Kingdom of Saudi Arabia, officially established in 1932. Islam continues to be the basis of Saudi society, politics, and law: according to its Basic Law (1992), the Saudi government's legal authority derives from sacred Islamic texts (Art. 7) and its constitution is based on interpretations of the Qur'an and hadith (Art. 1). In addition to the Basic Law, a system of legal opinions, state regulations, royal decrees, and local customs make up Saudi law. For the most part, Saudi law follows the Hanbali school of legal interpretation.

The majority Saudi legal opinion is that the entire body of a woman is *'awra* except for her hands and eyes. Accordingly, women in most of the country wear a face-veil, headcovering, and full black cloak called *abaya* when in public. Although there is no single national law that stipulates the Saudi dress code, the obligation to cover in public is enforced by the Committee for the Promotion of Virtue and The Prevention of Vice who rely on the religious police (*mutawwa'in*). The unwritten nature of the Saudi legal dress code makes it no less enforceable. Even non-Muslim visitors to Saudi Arabia must cover. In fact, Saudi Arabia is the only country where the US military has required female personnel to wear the *abaya*. This uncodified status is similar to the driving ban for women in Saudi Arabia, which was strictly enforced even before legislation was drafted and ratified in 1990.

One advantage to the fact that Saudi veiling law is mostly unwritten is that this gives judges significant discretionary power, which they usually exercise in favor of local customs. For this reason veiling practice and regulation varies by region. While in the capital Riyadh *abaya* is strictly enforced, in Jeddah women have more leeway regarding their clothing.

Afghanistan under Taliban rule

Under the Taliban rule of Afghanistan, a literal interpretation of the shari'a was combined with local Pashtun tribal codes and customary laws to make illegal a wide variety of activities. According to the prominent Pakistani scholar and Taliban supporter 'Allamah Muhammad Musa Ruhani al-Bazi (d. 1998), establishing a legal system based on an interpretation of shari'a was central to the Taliban regime: 'It has now become clear as daylight that only the Islamic laws [and shari'a based] penalties can guarantee in the world – peace, prosperity, safety, contentment, happiness, and progress' (as quoted in Telesetsky 1998, 295n224.) As part of these new laws, the Taliban imposed a mandatory dress code of a *burqa*, a full body covering with a lace opening for the eyes (see figure 2, page 8). A 1996 Taliban decree states, 'If women are going outside with fashionable, ornamental, tight and charming clothes to show themselves, they will be cursed by the Islamic shari'a, and should never expect to go to heaven' (as quoted in Rashid 2000, 217). Men also had a dress code: a beard longer than a fist placed at the base of the chin, short head hair, and a head covering.

Additional rules related to public dress were issued by the Ministry for the Promotion of Virtue and Suppression of Vice (PVSV), and strictly enforced by its religious police. Violations included white socks, shoes that squeak, *burqas* made of too thin material, and bare ankles. Punishments were severe, and often carried out publicly. In October 1996, a woman had the tip of her thumb cut off for wearing nail polish. In December 1996, 225 women were lashed on their legs and backs for violating the Taliban dress code. In 1997, a woman was shot by a Taliban officer for showing her ankles while sitting on a bicycle.

Despite the removal of the Taliban from power, Islamic law holds a place of privilege in the current regime. Although the PVSV was closed when the Taliban was removed, in 2003 the Chief Justice of the Supreme Court of Afghanistan reinstated it. In addition, article 3 of the 2004 constitution states: 'no law shall contravene the tenets and provisions of the holy religion of Islam in Afghanistan'. This means, in essence, any aspect of the civil law that contradicts interpretations of shari'a is invalid.

Summary

The system of Islamic law is fundamentally a system of diversity and change. *Fiqh* is not a cohesive unchanging body of knowledge, but rather an ongoing process that takes places within specific historical contexts and reflects local customs. Contemporary scholars of Islam have pointed out that in order for Islamic law to be relevant in a variety of contexts and ages, it 'must embrace the idea of an active movement in the construction of meaning' (El Fadl 2001, 146). Historically, Islamic legal thought has left room for contradictory opinions. It was common for even the same jurist to have different opinions on the same issue (Khalafallah 2005, 49). For this reason, the manner in which the Islamic veil was defined in legal discussions differs greatly over time and across space. Not only is there no single, universal 'Islamic law' about covering women's bodies, a search for such a law fundamentally misunderstands the nature of legal thought in Islam. We should always think of legal opinions on the veil in the plural.

One crucial influence that legal reasoning had on the Islamic veil was establishing the logical link between covering *'awra* and preventing *fitna*. It was medieval jurists who made mainstream the assumption that covering certain parts of a woman's body was necessary in order to prevent the sin of illicit sexual encounters. This logical move made preventing sexual arousal, versus enacting pious modesty, the primary legal goal of the Islamic veil.

The efforts in the nineteenth and twentieth centuries to draft Islamic legislative codes have also had an enormous impact on the Islamic veil. Because Islamic law was not a fixed code in this way for most of its history, it was up to Muslims to determine the extent to which they wanted to abide by Islamic rights and duties. This has changed in the modern period, when some Islamic governments began to legally require all women to veil in public.

Iran, Saudi Arabia, and Afghanistan are examples of modern governments that tried to base national laws on Islamic legal principles. They shared the assumption that all actions considered sins in legal thought should be crimes and punished according to specific penalties mentioned in the Qur'an (e.g. lashes, stoning). These governments relied on written codes, government decrees, Islamic judges, and 'moral police' to enforce a legal duty to veil.

Although all three cases are attempts to apply Islamic law independent of socio-historical context, the very fact that their codes differ is proof of the diversity of interpretation of what Shari'a says about the Islamic veil. These governments relied on different schools of legal thought (Jafari, Hanbali, and Hanafi). They legislated in different ways (constitutions, penal codes, and official decrees). What must be covered differed (heads and hair, bodies, eyes). Thus, the legal definition of the Islamic veil varied in each context. In contrast to a single vision of what Shari'a dictates for Islamic government in regards to the veil, these three examples of compulsory veiling demonstrate how local customs and historical contexts greatly affect the interpretation and application of Islamic law.

The function of law as a way to control populations is not a goal of pre-modern *fiqh*. For some critics of mandatory veiling, the practice is not only problematic because it is physically restrictive, but also because it interferes with the ability of women to use the veil as an expression of piety (chapter 1) or identity (chapter 7). Veiling as a practice of self-regulation or self-expression is difficult when veiling must be performed under threat of legal punishment.

4

Colonialism

Throughout human history, colonialism and the types of contacts and discourse it created, has been influential in what French theorist Louis Althusser calls interpolation: a process by which ideas are internalized and made one's own (Althusser 1971, 218–219). In the case of the veil, confronting how non-Muslims perceive and define this practice has changed its meaning for Muslims. In general terms, this is often described as an interaction between Islam and 'the West' (understood primarily as European and North American forms of modern life). Historically, this interaction with Western discourse, ideology, and norms has taken many forms. Some embraced Western ideas (e.g. Ottoman Empire and later Turkey), others ignored them (e.g. Persia and later Iran), and still others resisted them, as during imposed colonial rule of much of the Middle East. This chapter focuses on this last case, describing how colonial interactions between Islam and 'the West' during the twentieth century has left, in the words of the historian Leila Ahmed, the veil 'pregnant with meanings' (Ahmed 1992, 166).

Ania Loomba defines colonialism 'as the conquest and control of other people's land and goods', a practice she traces back to the second-century Roman Empire (Loomba 2005, 8). Juan Cole and Deniz Kandiyota suggest the colonial era for most Middle Eastern and Central Asian states can be divided into three periods – informal imperialism, formal colonial domination, and neo-colonialism – although the periodization looks different in each area. Some countries, like Iran and Turkey, did not experience the formal colonial domination period in any meaningful way (Cole & Kandiyoti 2002, 190).

European colonialism is the most extensive example of this conquest and control in human history. By the 1930s Europe controlled eighty-four per cent of the land surface of the globe (Loomba 2005, 3). This means that the majority of Muslims alive today live in countries that are former European colonies. Europe did not operate as a unified empire and the process of European Imperialism was gradual, and manifested through a variety of strategies, including exerting economic dominance, establishing military control, and leveraging existing internal conflicts for colonial advantage. Often European countries used the rest of the world, including Muslim-majority countries, as expendable pawns. At times this game-play was obvious: deals were often made between European countries over who should control specific areas.

When the Portuguese successfully sailed around the Cape of Good Hope in 1498 they paved the way for their own early control of the Indian Ocean, as well as greatly expanding the range of European ships. The British East India Company, established by royal charter in 1600, quickly followed suit and set up 'presidencies' in Bombay, Calcutta, and Madras in the seventeenth century. By 1857, Britain controlled virtually all of India and did so until 1947. During this time, France and Britain jockeyed for control of the important Egyptian rail and water (the Suez Canal) trade routes. In 1875 Britain gained the upper hand when reliance on foreign investment forced the Egyptian ruler to sell his shares of the Suez Canal to Britain. Britain declared Egypt a 'protectorate' during World War I and Egypt did not gain independence until 1952. Iraq was not colonized by the British until World War I, but it experienced a long period of neo-colonialism that lasted until at least 1958 (Cole & Kandiyoti 2002, 190).

France was also a major European colonial power. It invaded Algeria in 1830, beginning a long period of formal colonial domination that did not end until 1962. In 1904, France gained control of Morocco through an imperial deal: Britain, Spain, and Italy agreed to let France control the majority of Morocco in exchange for France letting Britain control Egypt, Italy control Libya, and Spain retain influence over north-western Morocco. Another agreement between European powers, the 1919 Treaty of Versailles that ended World War I, granted France control over Syria. This occupation continued until France was itself occupied by Nazi Germany in World War II.

Further east, the Dutch state took control of Indonesia from the Portuguese in 1816. Apart from a brief interruption by the French and Japanese, the Netherlands remained in control of Indonesia until its independence in 1945. Britain controlled Malaysia from the mid-nineteenth century until Malaysian independence in 1957.

Europe was not the only imperial power in Muslim-majority regions: the Russian Empire, and later the Soviet Union, was a major colonial player in Central Asia. And while Czarist control of the area of Central Asia known as Turkestan in the 1860s had goals, scope, and tactics similar to French colonial projects in North Africa, the time of Soviet rule (1917–1991) left its own complicated legacy on the development of nationalism in this region, especially on the role of Islam in the public sphere (see discussion in chapter 6 about Tajikistan).

After explaining general mechanisms by which colonialism affected the veil, I briefly describe three cases – Egypt, Algeria, and Palestine – in which non-Islamic discourses and occupations shaped the local Islamic meanings of the veil. My goal is to demonstrate that what the Islamic veil means is not a question that gets worked out by Muslims in isolation. Rather, Muslim experiences with specific, concrete, and historical events, including non-Muslim critiques of veiling, influenced the contemporary meaning of the veil.

Mechanisms of colonial rule

The ways in which foreign powers attempt to control, rule, and change local populations is the focus of much scholarship, a survey of which is outside the scope of this book. Instead, I limit myself here to the role of religion, women, and finally the veil itself in these strategies for governing indigenous populations, and identify three general mechanisms of rule: attempting to change the social and cultural role of Islam for political ends; linking women's status to the status of the nation; and targeting the veil as a way to 'civilize' local women and solidify colonial power.

Politicizing Islam

Empires thought the success of the colonial project required local acceptance of a 'proper' role for religion in society and politics. At the same time, Islam was assumed to be the defining feature of indigenous populations: the characteristic that made 'them' so different from 'us'. As a result, all problematic aspects of the colony, that is, those customs and beliefs that resisted the colonial project, were labeled Islamic and Islam became the focus of many colonial reforms in Muslim majority colonies.

The European occupier's view of Islam not only erroneously assumed it was a fixed, static ideology and way of life, incompatible with modernity, but also that Islam determined all political affiliations and allegiances of Muslims. This both over-estimated the effect of Islam on local life and under-estimated its ability to change and conform to modern ways of life. This political conception of Islam also had an enormous effect on how the occupiers viewed the veil, which they identified as a symbol of local backwardness and resistance to civilizing programs.

The colonial experience changed Islam for Muslims too. Once Islam was identified as the source of resistance to modern politics, being Muslim became not only a cultural and religious identity, but also a political identity and therefore a resource for nationalist struggles. For example, long after the Algerian War, Islamists drew on thinkers such as Ibn Taymiyya (d. 1328) and Said Qutb (d. 1966) for methods to make Algerians 'more Islamic' in an attempt to seize political power. For the colonizer and colonized alike, the colonial experience linked Islam to the political future of the nation in new and enduring ways.

Women as bearers of tradition

In addition to a focus on policing public religiosity, colonization is the historical moment when women's status becomes accepted as the primary symbol of how 'traditional' a population is. For one, women were the primary child-rearers, and thus hugely influential on future citizens. But there was more at stake: during this time, women came to be seen by both the colonizers and the colonized as the depository of all culture (including Islam) so that a nation would only be as modern as its women. This meant the limitations on Muslim women's public roles, rights, and education were used to justify imposing European civilization. One colonial policy even suggested that French men should marry Algerian women, as 'it is through women that we can get hold of the soul of a people' (Scott 2007, 55).

Women were not, however, passive bystanders in these debates. There is a large body of scholarly literature that analyzes women's active participation in shaping the new modern woman in colonial contexts (e.g. Abu-Lughod 1998). Women, like men, borrowed some aspects of colonial discourses and rejected others in their own struggle to determine what a modern Muslim woman should look like. Whether or not they bought into the idea that women were the bearers of tradition, they took advantage of the new prominence of 'the woman question' in political discourse to voice their own preferences for specific reforms.

However, despite women's attempts to advocate for themselves, their bodies became the site on which conflict between the male colonizer and male colonized was fought. Both assumed a connection between land, the nation, and women. Both attempted to remake women as the first step to remaking the nation. And both rarely took women's own preferences into account.

Veil as a target of reform

For many colonists, unveiling Muslim women was the first step towards civilizing them. For one, the veil was seen as a visual barrier that interfered with a colonial power's ability to control female subjects. The veil, in other words, was a literal obstacle to the modernization of the nation. Second, since the West's understanding of Islam was often based on superficial, biased, and surface impressions, colonists too easily equated veiling with patriarchy and the subordination of women. This allowed them to make a feminist argument for unveiling (in order to save Muslim women from Muslim men). Finally, since one goal of the colonial project was to establish colonial visions about what is right, true, and modern, the veil was read as a sign of rejection of this moral project.

Although some colonized women did tie the Islamic veil to their vision for the nation, by either embracing or rejecting it (we will see cases of both later), for the most part it was men who used the veil for their own political ends. The historian Margot Badran, for instance, argues that unveiling was never any central part of the Egyptian feminist movement, despite male Egyptian lawyer Qasim Amin's claim that unveiling was the first and necessary step to women's emancipation. In the nationalist struggles we consider in the next section, the veil was not a symbol of women's status chosen by Muslim women (in contrast to bloomers and bras as chosen by American feminists). The veil became politically significant only through the ideological fights between men.

The goal of colonizing an area was to remake local populations into modern, civilized, Western citizens, which required an acceptance of the entire Western vision of modern life. In the early nineteenth century, empires assessed local populations in terms of their political institutions and the use of technology. However, by the late nineteenth and early twentieth century, religion and the status of women became the barometer for underdevelopment and the justification for outside occupation and rule. The veil, as an easily identifiable symbol, became both a target of colonial reform and, as we will see in the case studies that follow, a method of resistance to occupation.

Three cases of symbolic interaction

The interactions of colonial and nationalist discourses do not follow a single pattern, and therefore the best way to understand their impact on the veil is to look at actual case studies. I focus here on the occupation and struggle for liberation in Egypt, Algeria, and Palestine. In all three cases the Muslim community was confronted with foreign ideas about modernity, religion, and gender, and yet we find in each a unique response which affected the meaning and significance of the Islamic veil in national politics.

Egypt: feminism as the handmaid of colonialism

The British Empire's occupation of Egypt began in 1882 when it was the largest and most powerful empire in the world. Although the veil plays a more central role in the independence movements of nations such as Algeria, Egypt is an important case study because it was one of the first places occupiers rhetorically used Islam and women's status to justify the colonial project.

At the time of the British occupation of Egypt, Egyptian women wore a wide variety of clothes, including a head covering and white gauze face-veil that came to be referred to simply as 'the veil'. This face-veil became a topic of wide political debate in Egypt, especially among the British occupiers. Lord Cromer, British Consul General who helped govern Egypt from 1883–1907, is a good example. In his writings he expressed a strong opinion of the inferiority of Muslim society as compared to Europe. For him, the fact that Egyptian women wore a face-veil was evidence of why Egypt needed to remain a colony. Veiling was 'the fatal obstacle', Cromer argued, to the local Egyptian population's ability to attain 'that elevation of thought and character which should accompany the introduction of Western civilization' (quoted in Ahmed 1992, 153).

At first glance, Cromer is making a feminist claim motivated by a concern with liberating Egyptian women: Islam is an obstacle to Muslim women's freedom, and the Islamic veil is the readily observable proof of that oppression. Two things, however, contradict this generous reading of Cromer. For one, the policies he put in place as Consul General did not actually help Egyptian women gain equality. He did little to encourage girls to obtain an education and he specifically deterred women from becoming medical doctors, a vocation he thought better suited to men. Even more telling is the political position he took on women's rights in England: back home he was a founding member of the Men's League for Opposing Women's Suffrage. Leila Ahmed describes Cromer's selective use of feminism in the following way:

Feminism on the home front and feminism directed against white men was to be resisted and suppressed; but taken abroad and directed against the cultures of colonized peoples, it could

> be promoted in ways that admirably served and furthered the
> project of the dominance of the white man (Ahmed 1992, 153).

In the case of Cromer we see feminism being rhetorically co-opted to support the political aims of colonialism with little real concern for women's equality.

Lord Cromer's view of veiling as an obstacle to Egypt's development into a modern nation-state was not an isolated occurrence. In fact, the same logic gets adopted by nationalists even as they argue against the legitimacy of British occupation. In his widely read book *The Liberation of Women*, the French-educated Egyptian lawyer Qasim Amin advocated for the removal of the face-veil in Egypt in lieu of the 'legal veil' that covered a woman's head. This modification, he argued, would be beneficial for the economy, because it would better facilitate business interactions between men and women. In addition he thought the legal veil more modest than a face-veil, which he believed revealed only the most attractive part of a woman: her eyes.

Amin's book elicited a passionate response in Egypt: over thirty articles and books were written engaging his argument, many critical. The global Arabic press picked up the debate as well, making the veil an issue of political debate within the Muslim community in a new way. Amin's critics point out that he adopted the colonial idea that the status of a nation is linked to the status of its women. In fact he spent substantial time in his book trying to prove this historically, concluding, 'When the status of a nation is low ... the status of women is also low, and when the status of a nation is elevated, reflecting the progress and civilization of that nation, the status of women in that country is also elevated' (Amin 2000, 165). Since Amin's concern with women's status was related to his vision for the nation, even the reforms he directed at women, such as increased access to education, were to benefit the nationalist cause: educated mothers would raise modern future citizens.

In addition, and despite some disagreements over which veil-ing practices should be allowed and which should be banned, Amin accepted a number of Cromer's assumptions about religion, politics, and veiling. Amin, for example, had internalized the juxtaposition of Islam and modernity in Cromer's argument, assuming that in order to be modern Egypt would need to become less Islamic. There were other options available to Amin, such as challenging Cromer's imperialism by countering that the West had no more of a monopoly on defining what a modern nation-state should look like than the East. By adopting the premises of the colonizer, Amin rhetorically reproduced women's subordination in Islam and the superiority of the West (El Guindi 2005, 68).

Thus far, the voices of women have been missing from this overview of Egyptian debates about the veil. This is not an oversight. The veil became an important symbol in national debates for both Muslim and non-Muslim men alike, with little input from women themselves, who did not necessarily consider the veil as a symbol in the same way. Badran has vehemently denied that removing the veil was important to the Egyptian women's movement. In fact, upper middle class women were able to use the veil to gain access to public spaces and thus fully participate in national politics. Leading feminists such as Huda Sha'rawi (d. 1947) and Bahithat Al-Badiya (aka Malak Hefni Nassef d. 1918) continued to veil. As Al-Badiya put it, 'we know veiling will not last forever' (quoted in Badran 1995, 67), but she made other issues a priority in her feminist political activities. The veil was even less of a problem in the rural areas of Egypt, where women did not cover their faces for practical reasons relating to daily labor.

When veiling did gain prominence among Egyptian feminists after independence, it was taken up as a symbol of gender inequality, not nationalist resistance to Western domination. By the 1920s Egyptian women realized that their liberation was not a significant part of nationalist projects. It was at this point Egyptian feminist Huda Sha'rawi said the veil had become 'the greatest obstacle to women's participation in public life' (quoted in Badran 1995, 93). When she removed her face-veil in 1923 upon returning to Cairo from attending the International Alliance of Women for Suffrage and Equal Citizenship Congress, it was a protest against Egyptian men, not the former colonizer.

Algeria: the veil as means of cultural assault and defense

Under the leadership of General Marshal Bugeaud, who would later become the administrator of the colony, the French invasion of Algeria in 1830 entailed coordinated efforts of 'scorched earth' policies, massacres, and mass rapes, all in the name of civilizing the local population. According to the famous French political scientist Alexander de Tocqueville, colonization was intended to 'restore national pride' which had been threatened by 'the gradual softening of social mores' in the Algerian middle classes (de Tocqueville 1954, 335). In 1834 Algeria officially became a French military colony; and in 1848 its new constitution declared it an integral part of France. French settlement began in earnest.

France ruled its closest and largest settlement colony by an assimilation policy that sought to integrate local Algerians entirely into French culture. In practice, this not only meant introducing French ideas and values, but also purging from the Algerian people any obstacle to this process of acculturation. Islam was perceived as the source of all ethnic differences and problematic conditions of the native population and assimilation became a crusade against all things Islamic. Evidence of this is seen in the legal option for Algerians to apply to become French citizens only if they first renounced all legitimacy of the shari'a to rule them.

As in Egypt, the fight over the role of Islam in the future of the Algerian state had particular ramifications for women. The veil was seen as an especially difficult obstacle to assimilating local women. General Bugeaud complained the locals 'elude us because they conceal their women from our gaze' (quoted in Scott 2007, 55). The veil was thus cast as a cultural symbol that needed to be eradicated in order to complete the process of acculturation. Unveiling would be the means to, and evidence of, successful remaking of Algerian women as French.

The irony is that although the majority of Algerians had been Muslim since the eighth century, before this colonial narrative about the importance of Islam, Algerians' primary self-identity was more often regional, tribal, or familial. However, once the French targeted Islam as the essence of what made Algerians different, Algerians themselves adopted this stance. By focusing on reforming Islamic beliefs and practices in order to control Algerians, the French actually made Islam more, not less, important to Algerian nationalist politics. Likewise, the colonial powers' fixation on the veil as the symbol of Islam also changed its meaning for the local population who began to believe that maintaining the veil was necessary to resisting French domination. Writing in the midst of the Algerian war for independence, critical theorist Frantz Fanon declared that part of the reason Algerians insisted on continuing to veil was 'because the occupier *was bent on unveiling Algeria*' (Fanon 1965, 63, emphasis in original).

The National Liberation Front (FLN) waged the war for Algerian independence, referred to as the Algerian War by the French, from 1954–1962. If the conquest of Algeria was violent, the seven-year war for independence, during which both sides engaged in guerilla tactics, terror and counter-terrorism, and torture, was even bloodier. Algerian women took a central part in this struggle through a range of combatant and non-combatant roles.

Thousands of women were foot soldiers, some of whom became national heroines for enduring torture and death at the hands of French forces. For the FLN, women's veiling was a symbol of their political allegiance to the liberation cause, and their resistance to French occupation. The veil also proved to be a military asset as it enabled the smuggling of contraband, as immortalized in a scene of the 1966 war film *The Battle of Algiers*.

The French tried to leverage the veil for their own purposes during the war. Part of French propaganda was that they could bring feminist liberation to Algerian women, and they targeted women in the hope that they could divide the local population. During one well-documented event that took place on 13 May 1958, the unveiling of Algerian women was broadcast on radio and TV. According to the colonial press, thousands of women spontaneously gathered in public squares to be unveiled by French women in a feminist protest against indigenous forced veiling. The *New York Times Magazine*, following the French spin of that day, described how French women 'lifted the veil from the heads of a number of Muslim women, who gratefully smiled at the cameramen' (quoted in Gordon 1962, 143). In contrast, the pro-FLN press described this as an orchestrated event in which French women unveiled their servants who were used unfairly as political pawns.

Whether this particular event was spontaneous or orchestrated, it is clear both sides used women, and specifically the veiling and unveiling of women, as a political symbol. 'The French chose Islam as the Algerian's common denominator and as grounds on which to fight them,' argues sociologist Marnia Lazreg, 'likewise, Algerians responded by making Islam the bastion of their resistance to colonialism' (Lazreg 1990, 759). Similar linkages of Islam and the Islamic veil to 'French resistance' and veiled women to Islam remain prominent in cultural debates in contemporary France (see chapter 6).

Palestine: the veil as a sign of emerging national identity

Great Britain might regret that The League of Nations ever officially granted them a mandate over Palestine in 1922 because it was such a troublesome British colony. Non-Jewish Palestinians revolted in 1920, 1929, and 1936. The local Jewish population continued to increase and by the 1940s Zionist activists wanted Britain out of Palestine as well. In 1947, after World War II, the British government voluntarily gave up its control of the area and the United Nations partitioned the territory. But things did not get easier in the region for Palestinians. A civil war began. Israel was declared a state in 1948, and by 1967 Israel had control of the entire area that had been part of the British Palestinian mandate.

Crucial to understanding the role of the Islamic veil in recent Palestinian politics is putting it in the context of the evolution of Palestinian national consciousness. Rashid Khalidi traces Palestinian nationalism back to the late nineteenth century, but notes that it was not until the British took formal control of the area that Palestinians began to imagine themselves as part of a single community (Khalidi 1997). Some scholars describe this emerging conscious as a reaction to Zionism (e.g. Shipler 2002), but Khalidi and others have argued that the first period of Palestinian nationalism (1922–1947) is better understood as grounded in anti-imperialism and as part of 'a universal process [that] was unfolding in the Middle East during this period, involving an increasing identification with the new states created by the post-World War I partitions' (Khalidi 1997, 20). In fact, although the majority of Palestinians are Sunni Muslim (ninety per cent), it was not until the 1980s that political Islam became a defining ideological feature of Palestinian nationalism.

Things changed dramatically with the June 1967 War and subsequent Israeli occupation, economic integration, and settlement of the West bank and Gaza Strip. More Palestinians became refugees or lived under Israeli rule than ever before. During this time, Palestinian nationalism refocused on the local Palestinian-Israeli clash, and political Islam, as a way to differentiate Palestinians from Israelis, became a more important ideology. This shift can be seen in the increased influence of Muslim groups like Hamas, as well as the new political role of the veil.

Intifada is the term used to describe the Palestinian action against Israeli forces from 1987–1992. While not a classic nationalist movement against colonial domination as in Egypt and Algeria, the Intifada was a resistance movement against a perceived foreign occupation accompanied by a politicization of Islam. As in the other case studies, this uprising had a tremendous effect on the local meaning of the veil.

The Intifada's underlying goal was to protest Israeli politics of detention, housing demolitions, and deportations, although the immediate catalyst was the death of four Palestinians at the hands of an Israeli truck driver. A mass riot broke out. During this Intifada, almost as many Palestinians were killed by other Palestinians – as potential collaborators – as were killed at the hands of Israeli forces. Proving allegiance to the Palestinian cause became literally an issue of life and death.

Rema Hammami is one of the few scholars to write on the significance of the Islamic veil in these inner-Palestine conflicts. She points out that prior to the Intifada, Palestinian women wore a variety of forms of the veil for many different reasons. In the 1970s a new form of the Islamic veil, insofar as it had no precedence in indigenous dress, was encouraged by the group that now calls itself Hamas. Called 'shari'a dress', this form of Islamic dress included not only a head covering, but also long, plain tailored overcoats. In the early 1980s, pressure to wear 'shari'a dress' was context specific: some places of work and some university campuses required it. But by 1988, just one year into the Intifada, it was impossible for women to walk around in

Gaza unveiled without risk of harassment (Hammani 1990, 27). This 'Intifada *hijab*' was not only about modesty or religiosity. It was also a marker of political allegiance.

What changed in those few years was Hamas' successful campaign to make the Islamic veil a sign of political commitment to the Intifada. Hamas published a manifesto calling for women to abide by 'shari'a dress'. Graffiti popped up all over the strip commanding the same thing. Groups of youths patrolled the streets harassing unveiled women. In a well-known case, vigilantes broke in to Ahmad Shawqi School in Gaza and attacked schoolgirls for not wearing headscarves. Although Hamas distanced itself from youths who attacked women, blaming the most violent attacks on Israeli forces and collaborators, suddenly any woman who was unveiled in public was viewed as anti-nationalist, pro-Israeli, and a symbolic, if not actual, political collaborator with Israeli forces.

The Unified Leadership (UNLU) finally denounced the harassment of unveiled women in 1990 (sec. 3 *bayan* #43). The same statement, however, also stresses the importance of modest dress (sec. 1). Since 1990, new campaigns attempting to impose not only head covering, but also full-length dress, have been reported (Hammami 1990, 27–28).

Summary

During colonization and decolonization of Muslim majority regions, particular interactions between occupying powers and local populations made Islam more important to emerging forms of nationalism. During this process, the veil, in particular, took on new significance through discourse about religion, gender, and modernity.

Three important points emerge. First, colonial empires were concerned with veiling, which they interpreted as a sign of underdevelopment. The occupiers' discourse on the veil also affected local understanding of veiling. Resistance narratives reproduced the idea of the Islamic veil as a symbol of the status of women and the status of Islam in politics in general. Even those who rejected the idea that women had to be unveiled to be modern adopted the premise that veiling epitomized Islamic culture. As Leila Ahmed puts it, the colonized population 'reappropriated, in order to negate them, the symbolic terms of the originating narrative' (Ahmed 1992, 163–164). This reappropriation marked a significant shift in Islamic discourse about the veil in many regions, and the veil gained new powerful cultural and political symbolic meanings in this historical period.

Second, although women were active in nationalist debates and independence movements, even taking on combatant roles, when it came to veiling debates, women were for the most part pawns in the political battles of men. The issue of veiling in these debates had little to do with women's virtue or veiling's religious meanings. Rather the veil was conceptualized as a political tool to be fought over, leveraged, and manipulated by men on both sides. Women in general were either indifferent to veiling or considered it an issue of gender equality, not a litmus test for patriotism or modernity.

Third, during colonization the veil became an important political symbol, but the content of that symbol differed across contexts. In Egypt the colonialists identified the veil as anti-modern, and some nationalists also began to see the face-veil as a sign of Egypt's under-development. Under colonial rule in Algeria, the French saw the veil as a symbol of resistance to their assimilation policies; for Algerians, the veil became a potential antidote to imperial domination. During the Intifada, the veil became a sign of allegiance to Palestinian liberation and unveiling a sign of collaboration with Israeli occupation. Islamic veiling functioned simultaneously as a practice that was regulatory and emancipatory, controlling and liberating, even within the same national context. If the veil became 'pregnant with meanings' (Ahmed 1992, 166) because of colonial encounters, these meanings vary between different people in different places in different historical contexts.

In order to help put into perspective the next few chapters it is also important to say a few words about colonial influence on the modern rise of political Islam in general. It is not only the veil that obtained new political significance during this time: the experience of external control and occupation by the West encouraged the rise of a form of Islamic activism called political Islam (and less accurately referred to as fundamentalism by the media and secular politicians). Political Islam emphasizes that Islam is a complete system for human life – not merely a set of beliefs and rituals – with values that should organize all aspects of life: personal, social, economic, and political (Sonn 2010, 152). Advocates of political Islam want to return to the golden age of Islam's glory and strength by replacing the foreign models of governance installed through colonialism with what they view to be more authentically Islamic governments. One of the most-widespread examples of political Islam is the Muslim Brotherhood, which began in the 1920s in Egypt and has become influential throughout the Middle East. The group's founder, Hassan al-Banna (d. 1949), made emotional appeals to Muslims' sense of humiliation from being colonized. In the words of its important member Said Qutb (d. 1966), the Muslim brotherhood solution was a complete return to the Islam, which 'is capable of solving our basic problems, of granting us a comprehensive social justice, of restoring for us justice in government, in economics, in opportunities and in punishment'. Having colonialism to blame for all social and economic woes made politicizing Islam more appealing.

Ironically, radical forms of political Islam do not easily cohere with Islamic nationalism. Although some Islamists do support a vision of Islamic government based on the shari'a, all supporters of political Islam maintain that sovereignty belongs to God, not the nation. As professor of politics and Middle Eastern studies Farhad Kazemi puts it, 'the Rousseasian idea of a social contract with its explicit acceptance of people's sovereignty has no place among diehard Islamists' (Kazemi 2002, 44). In other words, there is an ideological tension between political Islamist universalist messages and the particular realities of Islamic national movements.

5
Employment

One assumption grounding the modernization policies discussed in the last chapter was that Islamic veiling should disappear with economic development and subsequent advancement of women. Throughout most of the twentieth century, sociologists of religion also predicted the increasing privatization of religion in the modern world and thus the decline of public symbols of religious affiliation such as the veil. However, veiling actually increased in the 1970s, 1980s, and 1990s in a number of regions (Ahmed 2011). This was a surprise to many Muslims themselves, who see these new veiling movements as throw-backs to an older form of Islam.

What is confounding, even to many Muslims, is that many newly veiled women are educated, urban, and career oriented. They choose to take up the veil over the objections of their families, marking a generational divide. For these women, the veil is more than mere clothing. It becomes a type of portable gender seclusion and thus enables entry into the public sphere, not withdrawal from it. These women challenge both the liberal secular idea that the veil is an obstacle to women's advancement and the conservative Islamic idea that veiling is tied to women's domestic seclusion (Göle 1997, 21).

When asked, women usually explain their decision to begin veiling in terms of personal piety (as discussed in chapter 1). If we dig a little deeper, past these declarations of 'spiritual awakening', it turns out that the recent increase in veiling has additional motivations and meanings, which differ within various contexts. This is not to say that piety is not at play, but rather that there are external pressures which affect the choice to veil as well.

For example, in some cases veiling becomes a way to negotiate, and sometimes resolve, multiple visions of what it means to be a modern Muslim woman. Chapter 7 looks specifically at veiling as an expression of identity. In this chapter, our focus is on how contemporary veiling has influenced and been influenced by rapid economic development and women's increased entry into the workforce.

Readers unfamiliar with Islam might assume that the tradition restricts women's employment. It turns out, however, that the idea of Islam as an obstacle to women's access to economic opportunities is neither justified in Islamic thought nor observable in the Muslim world. For one, Islamic law gives women equal rights to men in the sphere of commerce and trade. Although the early Muslim community did not have the same variety of economic opportunities for women we have today, many hadith reports discuss Muslim women making business decisions and contracts. The Prophet's first wife, Khadija, was a wealthy tradeswoman who employed Muhammad before they were married. In many ways, her financial power helped to protect and promote Muhammad in the early Mecca community. A well-known hadith recounts Fatima's legal battle for her rightful inheritance from her father, the Prophet Muhammad. These women show how common it was in the early Muslim community not only for women to own property, but also to assert their economic rights.

It would also be incorrect to assume that in the contemporary world, increased Islamization necessarily decreases women's employment opportunities. The Taliban rule of Afghanistan is an important exception, but this sort of forced seclusion of women is not representative of the global trend of increased economic participation of Muslim women (Bahramitash 2002, 270). In Iran, for example, women's employment exploded after the 1979 Islamic Revolution, in part because compulsory veiling outside the home made the workplace 'safe' for women from traditional

Muslim families. Women's employment continued to grow in Pakistan under the rule of General Zia. In Saudi Arabia, where women have strict public veiling requirements, women-only work places are being developed.

There were general workplace trends in the late part of the twentieth century that set the context for Muslim women's employment. For one, during this time more employment opportunities became available. In the post-colonial Middle East, nationalist programs that drew from socialist ideology promised not only access to education for all citizens, but also jobs. Many of these new jobs were in bureaucratic offices, and governments have become some of the largest employers of the new working class. Corporations were another new employer in the twentieth century. These privately owned entities have their own sets of ideas about the workplace and their own self-image that they want to convey to the public. Both governments and corporations developed positions on veiling in the workplace.

Second, Muslim women face specific challenges when they take advantage of these new employment opportunities. There are logistical issues, such as having to travel on overcrowded public transportation where harassment is more likely. Women report that they feel safer commuting when veiled since it allows them to communicate to strange men that they are pious Muslim women. 'When I wear these clothes I feel secure, I know I am a good mother and good wife', Husnayya, a government employee, tells political scientist Arlene MacLeod during an interview. 'And men know not to laugh and flirt with me', she continues, 'so it is no problem to go out to work, or to shop, or anything. This is a good way to dress, it solves many problems' (MacLeod 1992, 543). New employment opportunities also came with social challenges for Muslim women, such as family and community pressures to make home, marriage, and children their priority. Scholars argue these pressures come from strong gender ideologies about women's role in the family, of which Islamic beliefs are only part (MacLeod 1991, 75–85; Hoodfar, 1997, 52–54). Every working mother will recognize the pressure to be both a good mother and successful at work. Veiling can be used to signal a woman's continued commitment to Islamic values of womanhood as she pursues a career.

Finally, even if veiling has facilitated women's employment in some contexts, veiled women face discrimination in the workplace. This is especially the case in regions where Muslims are the minority. Veiled Muslim women are transferred to positions with less interaction with customers, denied promotions, and fired because of refusals to remove headscarves. Once lawsuits are filed, courts become involved in the difficult task of determining if veiling is required by Islam, a task made more difficult by the fact that Islamic texts, legal experts, and practising Muslims do not agree on this issue. Courts often deny veiled women's claims of discrimination at work, even in legal systems that strongly support religious freedom. The legal reasoning behind such decisions has varied, but includes the assessment that veiling is an ethnic (Arab) not religious practice, and thus not protected under the freedom of religion statutes, or that veiling is an example of a religious practice that must be limited in order to not infringe on the rights of others. When courts side with employers, as they often do, the message is clear: women are forced to decide between work and religion, livelihood and faith. To make matters worse, governments are some of the worst violators.

The next section looks at three different contexts in which veiling has affected Muslim women's employment. The case of veiling and employment most widely studied by scholars is Egypt, where veiling in the 1980s and 1990s accompanied a resurgence of Egyptian women in the workforce. The media has often reported on women's economic challenges under the Taliban rule. I describe these challenges as well as how some women have found ways to support themselves despite employment restrictions. I also consider the impact of the veil on employment in the US, where veiled Muslim women have recently filed a number of high profile lawsuits against corporations for discrimination. These three studies show the range of ways veiling can influence women's employment. In some contexts, veiling helps women access new opportunities; in others, it is the grounds for their discrimination.

Egypt: resolving women's double bind

After a period of steady decline of veiling in the mid-twentieth century, veiled women suddenly became more common in the 1970s in Egypt. By the end of the 1980s, most women who worked in government offices covered their heads (Hoodfar 1991 & 1997; MacLeod 1991). Much to the surprise of some Egyptians, including older Muslim women who did not veil, women who began veiling in this time period were urban, held advanced degrees, wanted professional careers, and aspired to achieve middle class status. This 'new veiling' movement, as it has come to be known, was a demonstration of commitment to Islamic ideals within new employment conditions and capitalist aspirations. Today, approximately ninety per cent of women in Cairo wear some form of an Islamic veil, ranging from a head-scarf worn with Western clothes to fully covering the body (*jilbab*) and face (*niqab*).

Why did women begin to veil in Egypt in the 1970s and 1980s? In terms of employment, some similarities among the newly veiled women can be found. Most worked outside the home and therefore faced a double bind: they both wanted and were encouraged to work, and yet needed to prove to their husbands, families, the wider Muslim community, and themselves that they still adhered to traditional Islamic gender ideologies. Veiling was one solution to this dilemma as it allowed women to signal their desire to work in Islamic terms. MacLeod tells us that this is one point that the Carienne women she interviewed repeatedly made: 'This dress says to everyone that I am a Muslim woman and that I am here working because my family needs me to.' A veil allows a woman to deny her work is merely to satisfy personal career ambition: 'I am here because I love my family and we need some things for our home' (MacLeod 1992, 549–550). Anthropologist Homa Hoodfar argues that the new veiling among working women has practical advantages as well, including cost. One of Hoodfar's informants tells her: 'I wear a long skirt and this scarf. If I have only two sets of clothes I can look smart at all times because nobody expects the veiled ones [*muhaggabat*] to wear new clothes every day. This will save me a lot of money' (Hoodfar 1997, 118–119). Here we see the manner in which the Islamic veil helps women reconcile what might otherwise be seen as conflicting goals: middle class economic pursuits and Islamic family values.

Finally, the case of new veiling among working women in Egypt makes clear how veiling and unveiling take on different relationships to women's liberation in various contexts. 'The early feminist lifting of the face-veil [in the 1920s, as discussed in chapter 4] was about emancipation from exclusion', anthropologist Fadwa El Guindi argues, but 'the voluntary wearing of hijab since the mid-seventies is about liberation from imposed, imported identities, consumerist behaviors, and the increasingly materialist culture' (El Guindi 2005, 71). El Guindi goes as far as to call this new veiling 'feminist', because, and in contrast to the perception that veiling signals submission to the authority of others, in many ways new veiling is a rejection of traditional forms of authority. Other evidence from the Egyptian context supports El Guindi's claim. While Islamic movements have had enormous influence on contemporary Egyptian politics, there is no proof that the increase of women's veiling was the result of plots hatched by groups like the Muslim Brotherhood.

Women who put on the Islamic veil in the 1980s often did so despite their parents' objections and the opinions of powerful religious leaders, like the authorities of Al-Azhar University, that veiling was unnecessary. However, while veiling does increase women's mobility and thus access to employment, in some contexts it does so at the expense of reinforcing and reifying the norm of sexual segregation.

Afghanistan: the cost of seclusion

In September 1996, Afghan women's employment opportunities changed dramatically when the Taliban took over rule of most of the country. At the time, Afghan women made up a significant portion of the workforce: seventy per cent of the teachers, fifty per cent of government employees, and forty per cent of medical doctors were women (Dass 2002, 26). Chapter 3 described the veiling laws that came into effect with the Taliban's codification of specific interpretation of Islamic law, including the requirement that women wear a *burqa* (full body covering with only a mesh opening for the eyes) at all times when outside the home. The economic cost of buying and wearing this form of Islamic dress is not insignificant in Afghanistan, as a *burqa* costs about ten dollars, or approximately two months wages. Women are often forced to share one among family members, which further limits their physical mobility. Taliban laws also banned women entirely from the workforce. This employment ban had the unfortunate affect of denying women access to modern health care since male physicians could not examine female patients and female physicians could not practise at all.

In 1996, approximately 25,000 widows lived in Kabul alone – that number has now doubled – and the Taliban's ban on women's employment made it difficult, if not impossible, for them to support themselves and their children. Many Afghan women simply needed to work to survive. In some cases this meant dangerous unofficial work, such as begging or prostitution. The United Nations and other international private relief organizations became important sources of economic assistance to Afghan women. These international organizations continued to fund local non-government agencies, as well as local businesses like bakeries that employed women, even after women were explicitly forbidden from working directly with them by Taliban decree in 2000.

Other women successfully navigated the Taliban laws to run small in-home businesses in order to earn money from weaving, embroidery, and other handicrafts. Because of the ban on women's work, these women had their male family members sell any goods they made. Journalist Gayle Tzemach Lemmon's recent book, *The Dressmaker of Khair Khana*, describes the life of one such woman, Kamila Sidiqi. Trained to be a teacher, but unable to work under Taliban rule, Sidiqi learned how to sew from her sister and started her own business making clothes. She now employs over 100 women and runs an organization that teaches entrepreneurial skills to other Afghans (Lemmon 2011).

Few new economic opportunities have come to women under the Western-backed government of Hamid Karzai. Advocacy groups like the Revolutionary Association of the Women of Afghanistan (RAWA) report continued high mortality rates for women related to malnutrition, childbirth, and extreme poverty.

US: protecting the corporate look

Muslims in the US are facing increased hostility and discrimination in the workplace: formal complaints were up sixty per cent from 2005 to 2009 according to the federal Equal Employment Opportunity Commission (EEOC). Although Muslims make up only two per cent of the US population, they account for almost a quarter of the religious discrimination claims filed. While not all the claims of discrimination filed by Muslims involve women's veiling, many that make their way into mainstream media do.

US federal law requires employers to accommodate head-scarves unless doing so would impose undue hardship on the employer. Nevertheless, we see numerous complaints that corporations, in the name of promoting their own image, are steering veiled women to behind the scenes positions, not hiring them in the first place, or firing them for refusing to remove the veil. These actions often assume that customers are uncomfortable with veiled women, and imply that they are justified for being so. They send the message that the Islamic veil is not compatible with an American corporate image.

For example, a series of high profile complaints have been filed against the clothing retailer Abercrombie & Fitch, known for its young American, preppy, beachy image. No stranger to discrimination complaints, in 2004 this company agreed to a $50 million settlement with the EEOC over accusations that it promoted white employees over minorities in order to 'cultivate an all-white image in its retail stores' (AOL 2010). In 2010, the San Francisco bay chapter of the Council of American-Islamic Relations filed a complaint on behalf of nineteen-year-old Hani Khan. When Khan, who wears a headscarf, was hired to work in Abercrombie and Fitch's store in San Mateo, California, the store manager mentioned that the company's 'look policy' would require her to wear a white, navy, or gray-colored scarf. For six months Khan worked without incident in the store's stockroom, occasionally restocking on the floor. But a few days after a district manger visited the store in February 2010, and noted that Khan did not live up to 'the image' of Abercrombie and Fitch, an employee from human resources called Khan to tell her that her headscarf violated the store's dress code. 'I told her that is part of my religion, and that it is meant to promote modesty' (AOL 2010). When Khan refused to unveil she was taken off the work schedule. A week later she was fired.

Disney, another iconic American corporation, also has a record of discrimination against women who wear the Islamic veil. Twenty-six-year-old Imane Boudlal filed a complaint with EEOC in August 2010 when she was taken off the schedule of Disneyland's Storyteller's Café for refusing to remove her headscarf. Boudlal had worked for more that two years in the Disney themed cafe when she decided to begin wearing her veil to work. Disney officials believed her headscarf clashed with the restaurant's 1900s American theme, and they offered to transfer her to a telephone or bakery position.

According to Disney expert David Koenig, historically 'Walt (Disney) wanted people to be as friendly, clean-cut, and all-American as possible, and you couldn't stand out in any way' (Bly 2010, 10B). It is only recently that Disney's look policy has significantly loosened to allow female employees to go barelegged when wearing skirts, and male employees to have mustaches or cornrows. According to Michael Griffin, a Disney spokesperson, 'when cast members request exception to our policies for religious reasons, we strive to make accommodations', and he notes that 200 requests were accommodated between 2007 and 2010 (quoted in Greenhouse 2010, 17). But Boudlal refused the accommodations Disney offered her. 'I'm not a character in a role', Boudlal argued, 'I just wear a uniform'. She added that she would accept a simple and decent Disney alternative to her headscarf but was unwilling to wear the proposed cowboy hat version because in her opinion it is un-Islamic. Nor would she accept a behind the scenes position because, in her words, she would feel too 'humiliated' (quoted in Bly 2010, 10B).

Summary

Depending on the context, veiling can either facilitate or impede Muslim women's access to a job. Some employers (e.g. Islamic governments) require the veil of all female employees.

Others forbid it, seeing the Islamic veil as a sign of allegiance to principles that undermine a specific workplace ethos. Rather than searching for a simple answer to the question 'does the veil help women work?', a more subtle way to think about the veil in this area of life is to turn this question on its head to consider how recent global economic development, which has increased women's work opportunities, has affected the meaning and practice of the Islamic veil.

Some women have embraced the Islamic veil as a way to negotiate multiple pressures and ideologies. A veil can communicate that a woman respects her Islamic roles and values despite the fact that she works outside the home. It also encourages physical mobility which can increase a woman's access to opportunities outside the home. El Guindi reminds us that the voluntary veiling of working women (veiling not required by employers or the state) is the expression of Islamic feminism: feminist because it liberates women; Islamic because it assumes the validity of Islamic principles and values (El Guindi 2005, 71). Veiling can alleviate specific economic pressures. Many veiled women describe the savings and simplicity of owning two or three veiling outfits instead of trying to meet the expectations of a modern wardrobe that has a different outfit for every day of the week. Entry into the workplace is often motivated by a desire to obtain middle class status, but women perceive veiling as liberating them from the materialist culture of capitalism.

In addition, by participating in what scholars call new veiling movements, women are shifting the contemporary meaning of the Islamic veil. In other words, the veil is not the same thing, materially or symbolically, as it was just a few decades ago. No longer can we see the veil as merely clothing. And although as in other historical contexts – not only Muslim, but also Christian, Jewish, Greek, and Roman – the veil can be a symbol of women's seclusion, it no longer means confinement to the home when career minded Muslim women veil. Macleod has called this sort of new veiling 'accommodating protest'. It 'accommodates' insofar as it rearticulates the traditional Islamic gender teachings (mainly a women's primary duty to her family and the danger that her uncovered body can cause in front of men). It 'protests' insofar as it rejects the conclusion that this means women should not seek a career or financial independence (MacLeod 1992, 552). This accommodation itself, however, entails a tension since it expresses economic equality through reifying the norm of sexual separation.

These dimensions of the veil in contemporary workplaces all confirm a new conceptual and material veil. This new veil is stylistically different from older versions (e.g. veiled working women in Cairo wear a long skirt and headscarf which differs from the form of veil traditionally worn by Egyptian women), as well as a response to a new modern context. This new veil functions as portable seclusion, in contrast to older forms of women's seclusion that tied them to the home. The role of new veiling in the workplace demonstrates why unpacking situated veiling practices is so important: circumstances change, and the Islamic veil changes with them.

6
Education

Improving education, especially women's education, was central to many modernization projects in the twentieth century. These policies often assumed the same linkage of women's status to the nation's status discussed in the context of colonialism in chapter 4. Specifically, women's education was seen as necessary not only for women to become modern, scientific citizens, but also for them properly to raise children to be future citizens. Educational institutions thus became important sites for crafting citizens and ensuring the future of key political ideals.

Most schools have at least some rules about what students must wear – for example, shoes and shirts – and what things they may not – for instance, hats. But veiling in schools has recently sparked heated debates in many countries. Veiling is necessary to access education opportunities in some contexts, such as in countries with compulsory public veiling (e.g. Iran and Saudi Arabia) as well as others that require the veil to matriculate in some institutions (e.g. Indonesia). In other contexts, a student refusing to remove an Islamic headscarf risks expulsion (e.g. France and Turkey). In all these cases, the veil is the litmus test for young women's access to learning. In the mini-case studies that follow, we see how a number of factors, including anxiety over the increasing political influence of Islam, distress over the perceived oppression of Muslim girls, and concern about social divisions among students, has led some governments to ban headscarves in schools. At the same time, veiling in schools became a way for young women to protest what they perceive as the forced secularization and Westernization of modern society.

Attempts to ban the headscarf in French schools have been widely discussed by scholars, and similar political debates over proposed bans have taken place in other European countries such as the UK, Belgium, Holland, and Germany. However, this is not a phenomenon that can be simply explained by Western Islamophobia, as countries in the Middle East and Asia have had their own share of controversies surrounding veiling in schools. Bans on headscarves in public institutions have occurred on and off in Turkey since the 1960s. In 1993, there was a failed attempt in Egypt to ban the veil in schools. Azerbaijan, Albania, and Uzbekistan all ban religious clothing in universities. Tajikistan bans the headscarf in public and Islamic schools and universities. During Suharto's regime, Islamic headscarves were banned in Indonesian schools.

A number of normative tensions are at the center of bans of the veil in educational settings. First, there is a tension between the Islamic values of learning and gender segregation. While Islam puts a high value on education of both girls and boys, and sees learning and the acquisition of knowledge as important virtues, some Muslim thinkers teach that close interactions between boys and girls must be avoided in order to prevent social discord (see the discussion of *fitna* in chapter 3). When a young Muslim woman enters school, this often coincides with a new level of interaction with men. Girls may have to travel to school on public transportation or walk along overcrowded streets. Classrooms and college dorms mean close contact with the opposite sex. In some contexts extraordinary precautions are taken to avoid inappropriate interactions, such as using closed-circuit television to enable male professors to lecture to female students. In other contexts, the veil becomes a way to allow Muslim girls into integrated classrooms by supporting both the values of education and segregation.

There is a second tension between the ideal of a secular state and the demographic reality of increasingly multi-cultural populations.

Secularism can take a number of forms. The French version, influential in Europe and discussed in more detail later, considers all public religious symbols and practices threatening to the stability of the secular Republic. This form of secularism reduces religion to a set of beliefs and thus rejects that specific actions should be performed publicly as part of a religious life (see chapter 1). The veil is an embodiment of this tension. Since the late twentieth century, with the successful 1979 Islamic Revolution in Iran, the Taliban rule of Afghanistan, the First Palestinian Intifada, and the events of 9/11, political Islam appeared to be gaining global influence, and thus became a cause of concern for secular governments. This increased visibility of Islamic movements coincided with the appearance of more Islamic veils in public, including in some educational contexts. Veils thus became a focus for secular anxiety over Islam. Even if wearing an Islamic veil does not necessarily signal allegiance to an Islamic political party or movement, it is an easily observable symbol of the influence of Islam. As in so many historical cases (some of which have been discussed in earlier chapters), it became a convenient place to focus debate, and something that could be targeted in an attempt to ensure the survival of secularism. Finally, the veil challenges forms of secularism that consider religion a private matter. As a practice that must be public in order to have certain forms of personal, interpersonal, and social moral influence (see chapter 1), the Islamic veil resists secularist attempts to categorize it merely as a manner of dress or symbol of political allegiance.

Third, the debates over the Islamic veil in schools demonstrate the difficulty of ensuring the right to religious freedom and other fundamental human rights – such as the right to education and the right to gender non-discrimination – at the same time. The right to education is guaranteed by international law (International Covenant on Economic, Social, and Cultural Rights, art. 13). In order to ensure this right, states must eliminate gross discrimination in schools. Banning the veil in the classroom could be interpreted as such discrimination. Freedom of religion (International Covenant on Civil and Political Rights, art. 18) prevents discrimination on the basis of religion, but this does not mean citizens have an absolute right to practice in any way they want. States justify placing limitations on religion all the time to prevent the violation of other fundamental rights. For example, a common rights-based objection to veiling in schools is that it symbolizes women's submission to men, is thus a sign of acute gender discrimination, and therefore does not deserve protection. In this way, a policy that targets Muslim women is justified in feminist terms.

These three normative tensions – between segregation and learning, secularism and multiculturalism, and competing human rights – can be seen to operate in the following case studies. These cases allow us to see how various external pressures have concretely encouraged or resisted veiling in educational settings.

France: protecting *laïcité*

The French Veil Affair (*affaire du foulard*) is the most well-known controversy over veiling in schools. Since France's Muslim community of five million is Europe's largest, Europeans watched the events surrounding the veil in France with great interest as a possible sign of things to come as Europe's Muslim population grows in this century. In North America, the ban on veiling in France raised questions about the differences between French and American principles of separation of church and state. Global attention was demanded by the increasing tensions between French youth of North African descent (who the media often referred to simply as 'young Muslims' despite that fact that some were not practising Muslims) and French police, which culminated in a series of riots and arson attacks during 2005.

France was the first European country to actively recruit labor from abroad after World War II, especially from Algeria, Morocco, and Tunisia. This became an open door policy of immigration after the loss of the Algerian War (see chapter 4). Immigration changed further in the 1970s when families, as opposed to solely male laborers, were allowed to immigrate to France. The French recession of the 1970s contributed to social tension and fueled racism by creating the impression that Muslim immigrants were taking jobs from the native French. At the same time, the children of immigrants began to demand their rights to social services as French citizens, which was perceived by some French as putting further strain on an already strapped French government. Veiled Muslims became more common in public schools and the Islamic veil became the focus of anxiety over a perceived threat from Muslim immigrants.

The French Veil Affair is actually made up of a series of separate controversies that culminated in a 2004 law banning the Islamic veil from all French schools. The first incident involved the expulsion of three Muslim girls in 1989 from middle school for refusing to remove their headscarves. The second incident occurred in 1994 when the Minister of Education issued a memorandum banning all conspicuous signs of religious affiliation, including the Islamic veil, from the classroom. Between 1994 and 2003 approximately 100 girls were suspended or expelled from schools for veiling, although in almost half of these cases they were allowed to return to the classroom after French courts overturned their expulsion. In order to make the ban of signs of religious affiliation in schools more enforceable, parliament passed a law in 2004. Sometimes referred to as the 'veil law', it forbids the use of any 'ostentatious' religious symbols. The law technically covers not only Muslim headscarves but also Jewish kippa, Sikh turbans, and large Christian crosses; however, in practice it is applied almost exclusively to Muslim women who veil.

The European Court of Human Rights (ECHR) upheld
the legality of the French ban in 2008, arguing the French
government was ensuring 'the manifestation by pupils of their
religious belief on school premises did not take on the nature
of an ostentatious act that would constitute a source of pressure
and exclusion' (ECHR 2008, Art. 9). The ban has recently
expanded beyond schools: a new law banning face-veils, or *niqab*,
went into effect in France in April 2011. This law applies to
women in any public place such as schools, government build-
ings, courtrooms, hospitals, public transportation, and even on
the street. Police are instructed to ask women to remove veils
for identification. If women refuse they can be fined up to 150
euros. Critics, who point out that fewer than 2000 women wear
the face-veil in France, argue that the new law is President
Nicolas Sarkozy's attempt to exploit anti-Muslim sentiment for
his own political gain.

The primary rationale given for official attempts to ban
the Islamic veil is the protection of French secularism: *laïcité*.
For some readers, banning a religious symbol in the name of
protecting the separation of church and state may seem counter-
intuitive. This is because secularism does not take the same political form everywhere. For example, US secularism is concerned
with protecting religious institutions from state interference.
In contrast, French *laïcité* understands the separation of church
and state to be best maintained by protecting individuals from
the claims of religions (Scott 2007, 15). For French secularism,
acceptable religion is unseen, that is, practised privately. Any
conspicuous religious symbol is a challenge to *laïcité*, especially
in public schools, which are perceived to be an extension of
the state and responsible for forming future generations of
French citizens. In addition, the Islamic veil carries in the French
context a particular sense of defiance in that it acts as a reminder
of the failure of French civilization in the Algerian colonial context (see chapter 4). French secularism assumes French citizens

must give up the Islamic veil in order to prove their commitment to French republican ideals.

Political values beyond *laïcité* are at stake in the French veil ban, including universalism and feminism. In France, communalism (*communautarisme*) refers to the danger of prioritizing group identity over national identity (French theorists often cite American multiculturalism as a form of communalism that creates negative group identity politics). In contrast, French politics is based on universalism – the radical sameness of all citizens – which in theory supports absolute equality. Grounded in the principles of the 1789 French Revolution, universalism has encouraged a modern policy of assimilation of French immigrant populations, understood as making 'social, religious, ethnic, and other origins irrelevant in the public sphere' (Scott 2007, 11). The challenge of the Islamic veil, particularly in schools, is that it is perceived as a symbol of allegiance to Islam over France, and thus as a violation of universalism. This means that, ironically, French law targets Muslim citizens as a group in policies aimed at guaranteeing the irrelevance of group identity.

Twentieth-century French feminists picked up on these ideas of radical equality in their arguments against sexual difference. It is no surprise then that some of the most vocal critics of the veil were female educators. These teachers and administrators saw the veil as a sign of women's subordination to men and thus as a violation of their right to non-discrimination in the workplace, not to mention a betrayal of hard fought feminist ideals. In contrast, feminists in other cultural contexts, such as American feminist Katha Politt, point out that it is unclear how criminalizing the veil makes women more equal (Pollitt 2010, 10) and thus argue it is not necessarily in feminists' best interests to support the ban.

Finally, it is important to point out the racism implied in targeting of the Islamic veil, such as in the application of the 2004 law almost exclusively to Muslim schoolgirls. This can be understood as a legacy of French colonialism, which has pervaded contemporary French discourse on North African immigration. As described in chapter 4, during the colonial project, Islam became the explanation for what made North Africans inferior to 'real' French people. The modern French veil, in turn, is a symbol of immigrants' resistance to assimilation, and 'further proof that, whatever the technicalities of their formal citizenship, they can never be fully French' (Scott 2007, 88).

Turkey: banning the veil to protect rights

Today, approximately seventy per cent of Turkish women wear close-fitting headcoverings. According to Turkish law, these women cannot register at a university. Women who begin to veil after they matriculate face suspension or expulsion. University staff, including faculty, are also affected: they can be fired not only for wearing a headscarf, but also for criticizing or failing to enforce the ban.

As in the case of France, the Turkish ban is justified as a protection of national secular ideals. Turkey officially became a secular state in 1923 under the leadership of Mustafa Kemal Ataturk (d. 1938). Most Turkish citizens are Muslim, and Turkish authorities have always been sensitive to the perceived political influences of Islam. Extra precautions are taken in educational contexts to guard against the encroachment of Islam. State control of educational institutions tightened after the 1980 military coup and the subsequent establishment of the Higher Education Council (YÖK) in the 1982 constitution, which became responsible for administering higher education.

Throughout the 1980s, Turkish women protested the headscarf ban through public demonstrations and hunger strikes. YÖK's attempts to remove the ban in 1989 and 1991, however, were blocked by the Turkish Constitutional Court who ruled the bans were necessary to support Turkish secularism. In other words, the court denied that the religious beliefs and practices of the local population should be reflected in public institutions. To allow otherwise risked damaging the secular ideals on which Turkey was founded. In 1997 a military directive further compelled the Turkish government to enforce the ban of headscarves on Turkey's public campuses without exception.

The ECHR considered the right of young veiled women to matriculate in Turkish schools in 2005 when Leyla Sahin appealed her expulsion from medical school for refusing to remove her veil. In the majority decision, the court upheld the right of the Turkish government to ban the headscarf in schools to protect the 'rights and freedom of others', accepting the Turkish government's claim that women who wear the headscarf intimidate women who do not, in the context of a country where there are 'extremist political movements'. Citing earlier precedence, the court called the veil a 'powerful external symbol' which 'appeared to be imposed on women by a religious precept that was hard to reconcile with the principle of gender equality' (Leyla Sahin v. Turkey 2005, 2, 10, 111).

The most recent official attempt to allow headscarves back on campuses has come from the Turkish parliament, which in the winter of 2008 passed two constitutional amendments aimed at lifting the headscarf ban. Later that year the Turkish Constitutional Court again intervened and annulled these amendments on the grounds that they violated the principle of secularism as enshrined in the Turkish Constitution. Nevertheless, there is increasing recognition in Turkey of how veiling bans have prevented Muslim women from getting an education. Many universities do not currently enforce the headscarf ban, encouraged perhaps by a 2010 YÖK ruling against a teacher at Istanbul University who threw a female student out of the classroom for wearing a head covering. Significantly, an increased Turkish acceptance of the veil has coincided with both a heightened urban Islamization and engagement with the West: as upper class Muslim women migrate to the cities, they demand the right to veil, as do Turks who return from living abroad in Europe.

Although Turkey has modeled its secularism on European forms, the emerging meanings of the veil challenge this as some women claim the veil as a symbol of Turkish modernization that rejects Westernization. In contrast to following a European trajectory, contemporary Turkish veiling has strong ideological similarities to anti-Western veiling movements in non-European countries (see, for example, the cases of Algeria and Egypt in chapter 4).

Tajikistan: Soviet legacy and Islamic anxieties

When the Soviet Union controlled Central Asia, it repressed all public displays of religiosity, including the Islamic veil, in the name of communism. Even after its collapse, Soviet rule continued to affect how the new secular republics of Central Asia viewed religion. This is especially true in Muslim majority countries such as Kyrgyzstan and Tajikistan which, like Turkey, fear the rise of Islamic extremist groups who advocate for the replacement of secular governments with an Islamic state. The Islamic veil, which in this region is commonly a headscarf tied under the chin, became the focus of these anxieties.

In 2005, Tajikistan legally banned the Islamic veil in all schools and universities in an attempt to curb the growth of radical Islamic groups. In 2010, President Enomali Rahmon further instructed school principles to refuse to admit students wearing headscarves. Malohat Sobirova, a former university student from a village in southern Tajikistan, dropped out of college due to the hostility she encountered after the ban: 'It got to a point where

I felt like an outcast. I couldn't keep on fighting for my rights, so I had to go back home to my village … and now I'm unemployed' (Mamaraimov and Saodat, n.d.). The ban also affects the dropout rate for girls in primary and secondary school, which is much higher than for boys in Tajikistan. According to the organization Committee on Women's and Family Affairs (CWFA), which published a poll on women and girls who wear the Islamic veil in Tajikistan in 2011, more than eighty per cent of veil-wearing women have not finished secondary school and ten per cent have had no education at all (Nabiyeva 2011).

Tajik strategies to get Muslim girls back into schools have focused on reforming Muslim parents rather than lifting the legal ban on the veil. CWFA has programs aimed at convincing parents to allow their daughters to go to school without a headscarf by trying to 'convince the parents that their children must receive an education and that the clothes they choose for their children should not … take precedence over this' (Nabiyeva 2011). In other words, CWFA tries to persuade parents that the Islamic value of education outweighs the value of gender segregation. The Tajik Education Ministry is considering stipends and free textbooks as incentives to get Muslim girls back in the classroom.

Indonesia: recent reversals

Eighty per cent of the 220 million Indonesians are Muslim, making Indonesia home to the largest population of Muslims in the world. Until the 1990s, most Indonesian women did not wear the Islamic veil, locally referred to as *jilbab*. One reason for the historical rarity of veiling in Indonesia is that there is no local indigenous custom of head covering except among older women after they return from Hajj (the ritual pilgrimage to Mecca required of all able-bodied Muslims). Unveiling was further encouraged during President Suharto's 'new order' regime, which came to power in the mid-1980s. This regime assumed that veiling was a reflection of a type of Islam that could destabilize the government and banned veiling in government offices and non-religious state schools to prevent Islamic political power from gaining significant strongholds.

The national ban on veiling in schools was lifted in 1991, and veiling quickly became more common (Smith-Hefner 2007, 389–390). *Jilbab* is mandatory today in Ache providence, which unlike most of Indonesia, is governed by a shari'a-based law. Javanese universities have begun to encourage and even enforce veiling. In 2001, Universitas Islam Indonesia (UII), Indonesia's oldest private university, introduced new regulations requiring *jilbab* for all female students with the exception of foreign students. Four specific options for *jilbab* were introduced in 2005; new students are now mentored on how to wear proper *jilbab* (Warburton 2008, 4–10). At Universitas Islam Negeri in Yogyakarta (UIN), posters displayed around campus demonstrate acceptable versions of the Islamic veil (see figure 3). Even in universities where the veil is not required or encouraged, it is becoming more popular. When I visited Universitas Gadjah Mada (UGM) in 2011, over half the students wore headscarves in various styles, although veiled and bare-headed girls socialized with each other freely.

The status of the Islamic veil in Indonesia is an important counter example to the infamous French Veil Affair for two reasons. First, as in France, veiling practices do determine access to Indonesian educational institutions. In Indonesia, however, the veil helps women gain access, while in France it is an obstacle. Second, although the majority of Indonesians are Muslim, government support for veiling is actually a relatively recent phenomenon and was not the result of a local political Islamization. This means the status of the Islamic veil in

Figure 3 What to wear at Universitas Islam Negeri in Yogyakarta, Indonesia

educational settings is not tied to radical Islam as in some other cultural contexts.

Summary

Depending on the context, veiling can either facilitate or impede Muslim women's education. In some places, a headscarf will get you expelled from school; in others, it is required to matriculate.

Legal challenges to veil bans have increasingly involved secular national and international courts in the difficult task of defining the Islamic veil and working out a range of legal questions, including what actions governments may take to guard the political ideal of secularism. When these courts uphold bans on the Islamic veil, they rely on the interpretation that the veil is a symbol of support for radical Islam and women's subordination, thus privileging only its most conservative interpretations. As legal scholar Valorie Vojdik puts it, 'by conflating the veil with radical Islam, and assuming that women are political or religious pawns', courts 'erase Islamic women as active agents and political participants from the debate' (Vojdik 2010, 671).

Debates over veiling in schools expose possible conflicts between specific political ideals, such as secularism and religious freedom, gender non-discrimination, and the right to education. It is telling that some of the most heated debates have occurred in places with strong legacies of support for religious freedom. Human rights activists in particular have raised a number of concerns related to banning the veil. In a memo to the Turkish government in 2004, Human Rights Watch argued the following:

> Headscarves do not pose a threat to public safety, health, order, or morals, and they do not impinge on the rights of others. They are not inherently dangerous or disruptive to order, and

do not undermine the educational function. There may be specific circumstances in which state interests justify regulation of religious dress, as when such dress would directly jeopardize individual or public health or safety. Such concerns, however, cannot justify a flat prohibition (Human Rights Watch 2004, 24).

The veil will continue to be a human rights issue as economic development continues to create the need for educated, working women and thus new occasions and contexts for the veil.

7

Identity

Identity, an individual's sense of self or her group affiliation, is a fundamental concept in modern social psychology. An individual might want to embrace multiple identities: sex (woman), religion (Muslim), race (Asian), ethnicity (Pakistani), etc. The Islamic veil is a symbol complex enough to convey these different aspects of identity.

There are a number of tensions held together in the concept of identity that are key for understanding the multiple ways identity affects the Islamic veil. For example, identity is both individual and communal. It is understood as an individual attribute, but at the same time, an individual's identity is interactive and relational because it depends on others' perceptions as well as what aspects of the self groups say are important. Identity also defines in-group status. Barack Obama, for example, is commonly viewed by the American public as the first black president of the United States. He is considered part of the American black community, even though he embraces a bi-racial identity.

A second tension is between identity as something that is fixed and identity as something that evolves. Identity is perceived to be the aspect of the person that is constant throughout an individual's life. This durability and stability is what makes identity seem 'real' as opposed to arbitrary or based on a whim. Despite this perception, identity formation is an ongoing process. It is 'becoming' not 'being' (Dillon 1999, 250). This means identity is something that changes over time and in different contexts. Even the phrase 'I am a Muslim woman' can mean many different things throughout one person's lifetime: I was born into a Muslim home, I converted to Islam, or I pray five times a day.

A third tension is how a person's multiple affiliations are organized. In an article entitled 'Becoming Muslim', Lori Peek proposes that there are three types of identity, which she associates with levels of identity a person moves through during normal social–psychological development. Her categories are useful in conceptualizing the reasons for and means by which specific Muslim identities are embraced.

The first category is 'ascribed identity'. This type of Muslim identity is taken for granted insofar as an individual has very little critical distance from it. Ascribed Islamic identity is seen as 'natural' given a particular individual's circumstances, although it is not necessarily a person's dominant identity and may coexist with many different forms of identity. Muslim identity as ascribed comes from being born into a Muslim family and raised in a Muslim home.

A second category of Islamic identity is 'chosen identity'. Peek argues that a normal part of human development is becoming more self-reflexive about values and goals. This introspection can be initiated by a 'coming of age event', such as attending college or living outside the family home for the first time, when peer groups can influence a person in new ways. In contrast to the taken for granted or ascribed identity, a chosen identity is intentionally embraced after consideration of alternative options. If we take the example of Muslim immigrants, there are a number of ways in which religion can change from an ascribed to a chosen identity. A religious identity might have been assumed in the country of origin, where the majority shared the same religious affiliation. In a new context, where an immigrant is now part of a religious minority and thus feels pressure either to assimilate or assert his or her cultural difference, this identity may take on a greater importance. If this identity is retained it becomes a chosen Muslim identity.

Peek calls a third category 'declared identity'. Other scholars have called this 'salient identity', or the identity that takes on greater importance compared to others (Stryker 1980). How one identity emerges as dominant is a complicated issue. Peek suggests this often occurs after a 'crisis event' which inspires or requires greater critical reflection on one aspect of a person's identity. A clear example of such an event, which will be discussed in more detail later, is the terrorist attacks of 9/11. The event sparked increased discrimination and harassment of Muslims living in North America and Europe. Yet as difficult as this event has made the lives of many Muslim Americans, it also provided an opportunity for them to reassess and reassert their Muslim identity as a way to combat Islamophobia and convey a positive self-image (Peek 2005).

Because the Islamic veil is such a strong visual marker of identity, it is often assumed to convey someone's dominant identity. For example, when a woman wears an Islamic veil in a country where Muslims are a minority, others will assume she considers her Islamic identity to be her most important affiliation. We have seen in other chapters how a primary identification as Muslim challenges some political theories and can be seen as a threat to the stability of nation-states built on such theories. A clear case is French secularism, as discussed in chapter 6. Muslim schoolgirls' refusal to take off their veils is seen by some as a visible rejection of *laïcité* because it demonstrates that the Islamic identity of the schoolgirls is somehow more fundamental than French identity. The issue of Islam as a salient identity was raised in the UK after the protests about Salman Rushdie's novel, *Satanic Verses*. This novel, named after controversial verses in the Qur'an and containing fictional characters modeled on the Prophet and his wives, is considered blasphemous by some Muslims. Local protests alerted some British people for the first time to the potential for a pan-Muslim identity that might trump British identity and thus challenge political stability and cohesion.

However, given the complexity of the Islamic veil, the veil can mean many different types of identity – ascribed, chosen, declared – not only a dominant one. The mini-case studies selected for this chapter each highlight one of these three categories. Although the Islamic veil is often a sign of female gender identity, our first case is veiling as an expression of a male gender identity. In the Muslim Berber tribe of the Tuareg, all men of marriageable age put on a veil as part of the ascribed identity of an adult male and as a sign of male power, virility, and honor. The second case considers the decision to veil in the UK by second, third, and fourth generation immigrants. In this context, the veil becomes instrumental in the expression of a chosen hybrid cultural identity through mixing both mainstream fashion and apparel that references their countries of origin. The third case study considers the effect of 9/11 on the veiling practices of Muslim Americans. After this crisis event the veil was revaluated and ultimately declared a symbol of American Muslim identity. Women have in turn been able to use veiling to increase their participation in civil society. I conclude with a summary of some feminist critiques made of the veil as a marker of identity.

The veil of masculinity

This section borrows its title from a chapter of anthropologist Fadwa El Guindi's book on the veil that contains a summary of a number of male veiling practices in Islam. According to El Guindi, men reportedly veiled to ward off 'the evil eye' in pre-Islamic Arabia. There are hadith (e.g. Bukhari and Dawoud) that report occasions when the Prophet Muhammad covered his face, for example, as a sign of respect when he appeared before his father-in-law (El Guindi 1999, 119). We can add to El Guindi's examples Muslim men who occasionally wear women's dress as part of their ritual or gender performance. Dating back to the fourteenth century, the *bissu* are Muslim men in South Sulawesi who wear women's dress in religious rituals. Common still today in this region of the world are Muslim transvestites called *waria*, a combination of the Indonesian word *juanita* for woman and *pria* for man. According to anthropologist Tom Boellstorff, *waria* do not consider themselves women, but rather feminine men. This means that for *waria* who cover their heads, the veil is not the sign of womanhood but rather a male form of femininity (Boellstorff 2004, 161). These male practices of veiling, from the Prophet to *waria*, mean that the gendered identity conveyed by the veil is more complicated than simply 'Islamic womanhood'. This counters the widespread stereotype that the Islamic veil is always an expression of patriarchal oppression and women's subordination: since Muslim men have also veiled, this one-dimensional view of the veil cannot be accurate.

A closer look at the practice of veiling in the Tuareg tribe will help further explain how an ascribed male identity can be conveyed by an Islamic veil. In this Berber Muslim tribe, men, not women, veil. Known as 'the blue-veiled men' for the color of their distinctive dress, Tuareg men wear long, flowing robes and a head covering called *tagelmust* comprised of a low turban and a face-veil. Ideally, all Tuareg men wear this veil from the age of puberty, which marks them as being of marriageable age, until death. Veils are worn during all daily activities including eating, working, and even sleeping.

Tuareg men wear *tagelmust* in various ways to convey different levels of respect and politeness. It can be worn 'high' to cover some of the forehead as well the nose and mouth, in a powerful sign of male modesty and respect. This high veil might be used by a Tuareg man when he is in the presence of his elders or parents-in-law. When a significant sign of male modesty is not called for by the social circumstances, such as when a man is in the presence of his wife or children, the veil can be worn

Figure 4 Young Tuareg man wearing *tagelmust* 'low', Atlas Mountains, Morocco

'low' (see figure 4, p. 118) so that most of the forehead and all of the nose and mouth are uncovered (Rasmussen 2010, 464).

The Islamic veil is at its core a sign of gendered belonging and the veil of masculinity demonstrates how this gender identity is diverse and extremely context- and case-specific. In most cases the veil is correctly perceived as a sign of a female Muslim identity. For the Tuareg, however, the veil is not a sign of femininity at all, but rather of masculinity, male fertility, and male modesty.

The stigma of Muslim immigrants in the UK

Not all British Muslim women veil, and those who do veil do so for different reasons, including playing up or down different aspects of their identity. This section will focus on veiling amongst Muslim immigrants in Britain in order to explore the interactive nature of identity formation. The self-awareness of Muslims of their Muslim identity is heightened in areas where Muslims are the minority. One of the British youths interviewed by Kaye Haw for her project 'From hijab to jilbab and the "myth" of British identity' acknowledged that she never used to think about her Muslim identity until she realized she was part of a highly visible minority. 'I don't think you have to unless you go into a place where you are a minority. As soon as you become a minority you are forced to think about it aren't you?' (Haw 2009, 373). This increased awareness of being different can encourage, or discourage, the use of visual markers of identity, such as the Islamic veil.

Developing a strong, positive identity is a challenge to any young person, especially so for second, third, and fourth generation immigrants who feel caught between two cultures. They must balance maintaining loyalty to familial traditions from their country of origin and navigating the mainstream culture of their new home. This is made more difficult for many Muslim immigrants who experience a challenge to their British identity from other British citizens. Riffat, a young Muslim immigrant, describes the judgment a Muslim feels: 'They're thinking I'm a British person the same as this person but then I am not valued the same as that person ... I was born here and they're not accepting me – it's a confusion. I was born here I went to school here so why am I treated differently?' (Haw 2009, 373). In other words, although these Muslim immigrants are British, they continue to be perceived as outsiders because of their cultural identity: perpetual foreigners.

Turkish sociologist Nilüfer Göle proposes the concept of 'stigma' to explain why and how British Muslim immigrants continue to be perceived as outsiders. As Göle defines it, a stigma is an aspect of an individual that disqualifies him or her from being fully accepted by society (Göle 2003, 809). In the case of British Muslims, Islam is a general stigma that contributes to their social exclusion. For Muslim women, an Islamic veil is the physical manifestation, and easily recognizable sign, of this stigma.

The case of Aishah Azmi, a teaching assistant who was suspended for wearing a face-veil (*niqab*), is a concrete example of veiling stigma in the UK. Azmi's case gained nationwide attention after foreign minister Jack Straw used it as an opportunity to write a column in the Blackburn-based *Lancashire Telegraph*. In his column Straw stated that Muslim women present an 'apparent incongruity between the signals which indicate common [British] bonds' such as an 'entirely English accent' and 'the fact of the veil' (Straw 2006). In other words, for Straw the veil prevents British Muslims from being thoroughly British despite other markers of a British identity.

If the veil is a symbol of Islamic stigma, however, it can also be reinvented to recuperate the status of Islamic identity through the 'management of spoiled identity' (Göle 2003, 811).

Figure 5 Waiting for bus in *niqab*, Oxford, England

Specifically, a change occurs when the veil is worn as part of a 'chosen identity'. Much as the LGBT community has reclaimed the label 'queer' from its former status as hate speech, when a British immigrant chooses to veil as a symbol of pride in her Muslim heritage, the Islamic veil is recast as a symbol of prestige. Muslim women thereby effectively turn an undesired difference into a sign of distinction.

Emma Tarlo describes this change as a shift from being Muslim to being 'visibly Muslim', which 'is based on actions rather than origins. It is about how people wish to be seen rather than how others define them ... The category of visibly Muslim is open to anyone who chooses to identify with it, whatever their backgrounds or origins' (Tarlo 2010, 12). It is one thing to be born into a Muslim family. It is quite another to chose to be visibly Muslim, through the wearing of the highly recognizable Islamic veil (see figure 5). Göle calls this a change from being

'Muslim', which is something you are born into, to being an 'Islamicist', which is something that you choose (Göle 2003, 815).

The chosen identity conveyed through an Islamic veil is not always only Islamic. In the British context it is often a 'Muslim immigrant' identity, which is reflected in the hybridity of the fashion that Muslim woman in the UK wear. Young Muslim immigrants often creatively combine mainstream fashion such as streetwear with patterns, fabrics, and colors that reference their nations of origins. 'Their "Muslim looks" are concerned not just with issues of modesty but with particular aesthetic sensibilities to colors, textures and patterns which they consider to have an Islamic resonance' (Tarlo 2010, 41). Young British women wear long veils made of tracksuit material and also headscarves made of cloth imported from their countries of origin.

The choice of British immigrants to veil is very different from the ascribed veiling done by the Tuareg. For an adult Tuareg man, the veil is considered normal. These men do not make a conscious decision to veil once they reach puberty, rather they are merely fulfilling the expectation of the family and community that they will veil. In the UK, the choice to veil is a decision against the norm: the majority of British Muslims do not veil and do not expect their daughters to veil, and yet, their daughters choose to veil anyway.

The veil as icon after a crisis event

American Muslims come from various backgrounds. They differ in terms of race, culture, class, ideological commitments, education, and language, making them one of the most diverse religious groups in the US. The Muslim presence in the US predates the founding of the republic, but the majority of Muslims arrived after 1965 when the national quota system was replaced with other criteria for immigration, such as reuniting families, giving asylum for refugees, and bringing desirable professionals into the local economy. South Asian, Persian, and Arab immigrants currently make up over half and African American Muslims make up another quarter of the total American Muslim population.

A generation ago, scholars predicted that second and third generation Muslim immigrants would, as had been the case with other immigrant populations, gradually lose the commitment to their religious identity. But the opposite has turned out to be true. Some scholars have even argued that the US is currently in a moment of accelerated re-Islamization. The irony is that for many Muslim Americans it was after they immigrated to the US from Muslim majority countries like Pakistan, Saudi Arabia, Iran, and Bangladesh that they began to adopt visual symbols of Muslim identity such as the veil. Some Muslim American women wear the veil even when their mothers do not.

One factor supporting this increased commitment to religious identity is the value put on religious freedom in the US. Consider, for example, the American tradition of religious tolerance which, in theory, allows public religious expressions and protects individuals who are members of religious minority groups.

In addition, scholars have credited 9/11 as the 'crisis event' that has contributed to a more public embracing of Muslim identity in the US. Suspicions of Muslims existed in mainstream American culture prior to 9/11, influenced by the Iranian Revolution, first Persian Gulf War, and various terrorist bombings attributed to Islamist groups. It is undeniable, however, that 9/11 greatly increased American anxiety over the influence of Islam on American soil. This event linked, even if unjustifiably, terrorism and Islam for many Americans, which unfortunately resulted in an increase in harassment of Muslims. The Council of American Islamic Relations (CAIR) reported over 1500 cases of backlash discrimination against Muslims in the six months following the 9/11 attacks (Human Rights Watch, quoted in

Zahedi 2011, 188). Veiled Muslim women, as the most easily recognizable American Muslims, found themselves especially vulnerable to public harassment and the potential victims of hate crimes. Male Sikhs also became targets when misidentified as Muslim because of their headdress.

This difficult political climate also provided opportunity for increased critical reflection about Muslim identity. Some Muslims began studying religious texts for the first time in order to find answers for themselves about Islam and to help respond to public challenges against their religion. They reevaluated the issue of Islamic veiling, particularly its disputed obligatory status for Muslim women.

Within this context, some Muslims supported abandoning the veil, arguing that the veil was not crucial to Muslim identity and that it made Muslim women targets in the post-9/11 climate. Muslim jurists issued *fatwas* making it permissible for formerly veiled women to take off their headscarves. One such *fatwa* published in 2001 reads as follows: 'If a Muslim woman senses the possibility of danger to herself, adjusting her attire to minimize the chances of physical attack is a logical and Islamically permissible precaution that falls squarely within the *fiqh* principles of necessity and hardship' (quoted in Zahedi 2011, 190).

Yet even as some women unveiled after 9/11, scores of other women, particularly young women, put on the Islamic veil for the first time in a clear case of what Peek calls a 'declared' identity. This reclaiming of a 'damaged identity', can be interpreted in a number of ways. For some, this was an act of defiance against the increased Islamophobia in the American political context and a symbol of increased group solidarity. In the face of post-9/11 threats and drawing on the value of pluralism, Muslim Americans asserted their shared experience and identity, making the divisions within the Muslim American community less relevant. Reclaiming the veil also helped maintain a public role for Islam. As a visual affirmation of Islamic identity, it helped a public expression of this identity to survive. Finally, the post 9/11 Islamic veil is the public affirmation not only of Islam but also of the American values of religious freedom and tolerance. It is a patriotic act insofar as it expressed confidence that non-Muslim Americans will support Muslim Americans out of a commitment to religious diversity.

Although the majority of Muslim American women still do not veil, an increase in veiling in the US post-9/11 suggests that the veil has become more important as a symbol of American Muslim identity. This affirmation of the veil changes its meaning in the American context from a stigma as we discussed in the last section, to what Yvonne Haddad calls an 'iconic symbol of the refusal to be defined by the Western media and war propaganda since 9/11, and of affirming authentic Muslim and American identity' (Haddad 2007, 254).

This new status of the veil as icon has impact beyond issues of identity. For instance, it has allowed Muslim American women to become more politically active. Post-9/11 the Muslim community increased its outreach efforts as it tried to show Islam's compatibly with a pluralist democracy. Scholars have pointed out how veiled woman, as recognizably Muslim, have become important educators, leaders of NGOs, and participants in interfaith events. This means women have been able to leverage the veil as a symbol of Muslim identity to increase their public participation in a post-9/11 climate.

Critique of the veil as a marker of identity

The power of the Islamic veil as a marker of Islamic identity has a flipside as well: unveiled Muslim and non-Muslim feminists propose a number of criticisms of veiling for identity. Veiled Muslim women's own accounts of tensions that emerge when they use the veil to express Islamic identity confirm some of these critiques, so they are worth noting here.

The most obvious problem is that making the Islamic veil the most important marker of Muslim identity privileges one image of Muslim women – a veiled woman – over others. In this logic the veil is the salient sign of Islamic identity. This implies not only that non-veiled women are 'lesser Muslims', but ignores the multiple and overlapping identities of all Muslim women, such as sexual identity, national origins, race, and ethnicity. Rather than lumping all Muslim women into one homogenous group and reducing the essence of Islam to a mere form of dress, critics of identity-veiling would prefer that multiple images of Muslim women be supported.

Second, in many cases, veiled women are more likely than non-veiled women to be chosen to represent the Muslim community, which risks making the veil a *de facto* requirement for letting women become spokespersons for the Islamic community. As Pamela Taylor, a Muslim American convert, writes 'I am well aware that my wearing *hijab* gives me clout ... A non-*hijabed* [woman], especially a convert, is easily dismissed as not serious about her faith, as "corrupted" by feminism and the West. A *hijabed* woman has passed a litmus test and is not readily rejected by other members of the community' (Taylor 2008, 125). Sociologist Ashraf Zahedi makes this point even more strongly, claiming that 'many mainstream Muslim leaders and organizations had been hesitant at least, and downright oppositional at worst, to the possibility of a non-*hijab*-wearing Muslim woman speaker representing Islam' (Zahedi 2011, 199).

Third, although some women argue that they veil in order to prevent objectification by others, in some contexts once they don the veil they are perceived by many as simply 'a Muslim woman'. This means that rather than being accepted and assessed on her merits, a veiled Muslim woman must face all the negative stereotypes that non-Muslims in the West associate with Islam, including that Muslim women are oppressed, uneducated, and have no will or agency of their own. As Pamela Taylor, a veiled convert, writes, 'I cannot help but feel the bitter irony of having swapped one form of objectification for another' (Taylor 2008, 121).

A final feminist critique of veiling is that it is a male ascribed marker of a Muslim woman's identity, a legacy it can never completely rid itself of. According to Marnia Lazreg, the problem is that the identity associated with the veil is not free to be completely remade because it entails strong associations with power, politics, and gender. It is simply too implicated in negative politics to be successfully transformed from a stigma into a positive icon. 'I am not convinced', Lazreg writes, 'that wearing a scarf on one's head … helps to reduce prejudice against Muslims or elicits greater respect for them' (Lazreg 2009, 61). In the same way, she thinks it is not possible that the veil can become an icon that does not further burden women with assumptions about their 'biology and social destiny' (Lazreg 2009, 65). For Lazreg, the Islamic veil has always been, and will always be, 'a man's affair before it becomes a woman's' (Lazreg 2009, 57).

Summary

Many Muslim women veil to convey an identity to others, but it is not an easy task to explain what this identity is. As with so many other facets of the veil, its meaning is diverse. A woman who veils when she reaches puberty at the urging of her family, and has always taken it for granted that she will eventually veil, embraces a different type of identity than a woman who veils despite objections from her family, or in protest within a specific political climate. The cases of ascribed, chosen, and declared identity discussed have demonstrated that the veil is sufficiently complex to convey different specific identities in multiple contexts.

Despite that fact that many Muslim women claim their veils as positive expressions of identity, critics have raised concerns over the ways in which identity-veiling privileges the image of a veiled Muslim woman over other possible visual expressions of identity, as well as whether or not it is possible to use the veil in a way that is free from its negative gender associations.

8

Fashion

One has only to look around at the dizzying diversity of how women wear the veil, as well as references to Islamic head coverings showing up in collections of major non-Muslim designers, to know that Muslim women adopt, challenge, and set fashion trends. Veiling fashion includes both the wearing of clothes specifically made for Islamic women and the styling of non-specialized clothing to abide by Islamic covering restrictions.

Thinking about veiling as fashion, however, is controversial. For one thing, 'veiling-fashion' is conceptually difficult in that it seems to combine two incompatible symbolic systems: veiling, which references tradition and divine revelation, and fashion, which is ever changing, consumer-based, and decisively modern (Niessen 2008, 7). Some conservative Islamic groups describe this tension in more extreme terms. For instance, in an essay titled 'The Attack on the Veil', the international Muslim group Hizb ut-Tahrir (The Liberation Party) calls fashion 'man made, superficial and pretentious' and any discussion of Islamic fashion an 'insult' to Islam. They go on to argue that the motivation to cover for Muslim women 'is in complete contradiction with the desire to attain a specific appearance based on trends set by the fashion industry' (Hizb ut-Tahrir 2003, 20).

Despite these apparent conceptual and theological challenges, fashion and veiling seem to be easily held together in the design, production, and marketing of the veil, as well as in the actual sartorial practices of Muslim women. In contemporary designs, religious and fashion goals are simultaneously met through the use of traditional materials and the adoption of traditional forms in new ways. For instance, in Indonesia Islamic clothing made from batik has become more popular in the last five years, as the county reclaims its tradition of fabric production. In Europe and the US, the mixing of fashion and tradition can be seen in hip-hop veiling styles, which use hoodies and tracksuits to cover. There is growing interest in headscarves made from fabrics that reference older forms of dress, such as the robes of Ottoman courts, the embroidery of the Qajar Dynasty, or rural techniques of weaving.

Although the production of veiling fashion can be motivated by purely capitalist goals, it can also be justified in Islamic terms. For example, companies that produce Islamic dress for women argue that the number of women who wear the veil can be increased by making veils literally more attractive. Fashionably veiled women act as role models and inspirations for Muslim women who are considering veiling. Veiling fashion even has the potential to help overcome Muslim stereotypes by breaking down visual barriers between Muslim and non-Muslim women (Tarlo 2010, 199). A Muslim woman who veils using current fashion trends, like a maxi-dress over a long-sleeved shirt, can seem less different from her non-Muslim peers. She also expresses Western values of creativity and self-expression through her individual style. In these ways, fashion-veiling can make Islam more visually familiar, and thus acceptable, to non-Muslims.

The modern system of clothing production is a relatively recent invention. Prior to the mid-nineteenth century, most clothing was handmade. By the beginning of the twentieth century – with the invention of sewing machines and the development of the factory system of production – clothing has increasingly been produced on a larger scale. Today, global systems of production and marketing ensure the trans-national circulation of clothing. An article can be designed in one country, manufactured in another, and retailed in yet another. Veiling fashion is no exception and the Islamic veil is becoming big business; the veiling clothing market responds to Muslim women's desire both to wear some form of the Islamic covering and to dress according to the current trends.

Turkey has historically been the leading exporter of special-ized Islamic clothing for women; scarves made in China and India are popular and affordable choices for covering heads and hair; and the Middle East produces and exports traditional Arab versions of the veil such as the *abaya*. Women purchase tunics, long-sleeved base-layers, full-legged pants, long skirts, and head coverings in order to veil. Under-garments for the headscarves are also available to make the shape of the scarf more stylish. For example, in Iran you can purchase scrunchies made of fake hair, which create a 'bump' under the scarf. Turkish women can find padded bonnets that help them to create a fashionable bee-hive version of the veil. In Indonesia, skullcaps with a small 'bun' pillow, called 'bun' *ciput*, not only provide something on which to anchor a scarf with pins, they also create, in the words of one Javanese woman I spoke to, 'something more interesting to look at' (see figure 6, p. 132).

The economic cost of buying and wearing certain styles of Islamic dress should not be ignored. In Afghanistan, the required *burqa* costs about ten dollars or about two months wages which means that women often share one among family members. Wearing the Gulf style of *abaya* in India can be over ten times more costly than a sari. But in other places, women layer clothing from mainstream stores, so that wearing the Islamic veil, even fashionable versions, is not significantly more expensive than other clothing options. In addition, there are forms of economic impact for the consumer beyond costs. Fashionable veiling can convey economic power: it is a sign that a woman is wealthy enough to buy expensive, in mode, versions of the Islamic veil for herself or savvy enough to get financial contributions from her husband, family, or friends so that she may 'dress up' (Schulz 2007, 261).

Figure 6 Indonesian college student wearing 'bun' *ciput* under her headscarf, Yogyakarta, Indonesia

A common stereotype is that Muslim women wear what Muslim men, whether their fathers, husbands, or male religious authorities, tell them to. Most women, however, insist their particular veiling style reflects personal choice. We can accept that women choose a version of the Islamic veil based on personal taste (for example, a headscarf in a woman's favorite color or pattern), while at the same time acknowledging that a range of external factors influences these choices. Some women follow what their friends are wearing. Others intentionally conform to or protest societal norms. Prominent Islamic designers, storeowners, and bloggers shape what is considered 'in mode'. Women frequently admit to choosing styles that flatter them.

Muslim women often articulate donning the veil as a fashion opportunity: a chance to learn about fashion as they transition to a new wardrobe, or to wear an externally required form of dress to their greatest personal advantage. Women create 'Islamically aware outfits' (Tarlo 2010, 190) by drawing on their fashion skills. They know which base layers are the most flattering and trendy; they are able to play with colors and textures as they mix and match off-the-rack clothing; and they shop at the stores most likely to sell scarves, separates, and accessories suitable for veiling. And in the skillful hands of the *hijabi* fashionistas, women who intentionally create their own style, the Islamic veil becomes an art form: through layering printed fabrics, combining colors, and integrating traditional patterns, the fashionista skillfully drapes, twists, layers, pins, and accessorizes (see figure 7, p. 137).

The mini-case studies that follow look at veiling fashion in three very different contexts: post-revolutionary Iran, where Islamic dress is legally required of all women; post-Suharto Indonesia, where veiling has recently become popular after years of being politically discouraged; and South India in the 1990s, when an older South Asian system of *purdah* began to be observed by Muslims in greater numbers. In Iran, the Islamic veil held an important place through the twentieth century in struggles

Figure 7 Shopping for accessories, this woman is wearing a popular style of pin on the top of her square headscarf, Am Plaz Mall, Yogyakarta, Indonesia

over governance, whether it was banned by the Shah as part of his 'modernization' program, or required by the ayatollahs after the 1979 Islamic Revolution. In contrast, although Indonesia has the largest Muslim population in the world, women historically have not covered. The recent trend towards increased veiling cannot be fully attributed to an increased Islamization of Indonesian society or politics: it is also a fashion trend inspired by global secular fashion and veiling styles in other countries. In India, popular styles of women's dress have been dominated by Hindu cultural forms, namely the now iconic sari. Since the 1990s, however, South Indian women have begun wearing what is locally referred to as *purdah*, or modest dress, in greater numbers. Significantly, the forms of dress they adopt are defined against Hindu forms of gendered decent dress. Although politically and culturally very different, Muslim women in these contexts take veiling-fashion seriously. In terms of production, all three countries locally design and manufacture forms of the Islamic veil. In terms of practice, *hijabi* fashionistas in these contexts work to create their own veiling style, to catch the viewer's eye, to highlight their own special beauty, and even, as we will see, to comment on local belief and practice.

Pushing the limits of acceptability in Tehran

Women's Islamic dress, which is called *hijab* in Iran, became a major symbol of national identity during the 1979 Revolution when thousands of veiled women took to the streets to protest against the Shah. Veiling became legally required in national laws within four years of the Revolution, justified by the ethical teachings of Ayatollah Khomeini and other clergy, who argued that public un-veiling under the Shah had been a cause of immoral behavior and that public re-veiling would be a necessary condition of establishing an Islamic Republic (see chapter 3). There are two questions raised by the Iranian context. First, is individual expression through dress possible under conditions where veiling is legally required? Second, if veiling fashion does exist, does it have any sort of political power, even if unintended?

In some places in Iran, dress codes are specified, such as government offices and universities. Elsewhere, such as on the street, running errands, or socializing with friends in coffee shops, women can choose what to wear in order to comply with the law. The most common items used are *chador*, *manteau*, *maghnae*, and *rusari*. *Chador* (see Figure 2) is what often comes to mind when someone outside of Iran pictures a veiled Iranian woman, in part because it is an image of Iranian women favored by the Western press. It is a traditional form of Iranian dress, going back at least to the tenth century, comprised of a loose garment covering the entire body except the face and hands, often in black. The alternative to *chador* is a *manteau* with some sort of head covering. A *manteau* is a knee-length or longer coat, meant to hide a woman's shape. Two of the most popular head coverings are a *maghneh*, which is a piece of fabric sewn to leave an opening for the face that covers the entire neck, and a *rusari*, which is a scarf that is knotted under the chin or thrown around the neck, often showing more hair and skin than a *maghneh* (see figure 8, p. 137).

Given the range of options, what a woman decides to wear can communicate various things. For instance, a woman who wants to communicate modesty or her support for the Islamic Republic will wear *chador* or an extremely conservative *manteau* (dark, loose-fitting, and long) and the *maghneh* head covering (enclosing all the hair and fitting snugly around the face). In contrast, other women will choose a *manteau* and *rusari* which are brightly colored, tight, thin, or anything thing else that attracts attention (for example, capri pants or a lime green *manteau*). This form of veiling is called *bad hijab* by Iranian authorities

Figure 8 Schoolgirls wearing *manteau* and *maghneh*, Isfahan, Iran

(the Persian word for bad is *bad* so the concept *bad hijab* can be translated literally as 'bad *hijab*' in English). In many ways, *bad hijab* is a fashion protest against the control of women's bodies by the current Islamic regime; it is especially common amongst Tehrani youth of the wealthy, northern suburbs.

Bad hijab has been portrayed in Western media as resistance to local Islamic norms through adoption of Western concepts of beauty and sexuality into traditional practices of religious dress. And certainly at first glance many forms of *bad hijab* seem to imitate Western trends. When I was in Iran in 2004, particularly in fashion were what I called cowboy veils (with Western style stitching), military veils (khaki and dark green, sporting buckles and grommets), punk veils (dark makeup and piercings) and mod veils (with white piping and *manteaus* shaped like a Twiggy inspired mini-dress).

However, if *bad hijab* draws on Western fashion, it does not merely imitate it. The young women insist that their *bad hijab* practices are expressions of an authentic indigenous street culture. It does not imitate runway fashion but rather reinterprets and reproduces it for an Iranian cultural context. 'European styles do not always work here', one woman pointed out to me, 'because our climate is much hotter. Besides, we are fashionable enough to have our own trends.'

Importantly, *bad hijab* has political power in Iran, but perhaps not the sort of power the reader might expect. The practice of *bad hijab* is not 'feminist' in a liberal sense, because it does not necessarily change power dynamics between men and women, nor does it signal a movement of solidarity among women. Rather, it allows for the public expression of individuality and calls attention to differences between women. This aspect of *bad hijab* becomes culturally significant within a nation where seventy per cent of the population is under thirty and yet that same group has limited access to political office and faces high unemployment. The traditional forms of political and economic power are closed to them. Their form of dress is one way they have to draw attention to themselves and exert influence in the public sphere.

One concrete effect of *bad hijab* is perhaps not intended by the young women who use it, but is nevertheless observable to the outside visitor. Take for example one young woman my Iranian friends pointed out to me in a shop in northern Iran saying, 'Her *hijab* is so slutty' (see figure 9, p. 139). When I asked what they meant, one responded as follows:

> Her ankles are showing, her pants are rolled up, they are made of denim and tight. Her *manteau* is short, slit up the side, tight, made of thin material, and exposes the back of her neck and

her throat. And her *rusari*, look at her *rusari*! It is folded in half so that her hair sticks out in front and back and tied so loosely that we can see all her jewelry. Plus her makeup is caked on!

My Iranian companions were obviously shocked by this woman's dress, however their ankles were also showing, their side swept bangs were falling out of their *rusaris*, and none of them would have left the house without foundation, eye-liner, and mascara.

Despite my friends' reaction, this type of *bad hijab* has transformed the understanding of proper *hijab* in Iran in two ways. First, *bad hijab* shifts what is considered moderate *hijab*. In the past, Iranian women would be harassed or arrested for wearing anything except large, loose, black *manteaus* and headscarves.

Figure 9 Wearing *bad hijab* in Noor, Iran

Yet today, *manteaus* are short, tight, and come in a wide range of colors (including the brightest neons). Scarves are made of a variety of materials including thin, gauzy, semi-sheer silks and cottons. Forms of veiling that are perceived as extreme transform what is considered moderate, even for my friends.

Second, *bad hijab* has produced a tangible transformation in the enforcement of law. As discussed in chapter 3, the punishment for inadequate *hijab* in the Iranian Penal Code includes a fine, jail sentence, and even seventy-four lashes. But through their sheer numbers, young women wearing *bad hijab* make enforcement of the letter of the law impossible. There are not enough police in Tehran on a hot summer's day to arrest every capri-wearing young girl, not to mention the public outcry that would most likely result from administering seventy-four lashes for nail polish. When arrests do occur, young women are, for the most part, released to their parents with a stern warning and a fine. In this way the fashion trend known as *bad hijab* has shifted how shari'a is codified in Iranian law, changing the effective enforcement of the law. Veiling fashion has begun to form, instead of only being formed by, Islamic law and politics in Iran.

Indonesian conceptions of inner and outer beauty

The Islamic veil (locally referred to as *jilbab*) has only become common in Indonesia in the last ten years. Dress codes vary by region: in western Sumatra shari'a law makes veiling legally required, but in most of Indonesia women are free to choose if and how they will veil. Women who wear *jilbab* tend to cover their heads, necks, bosoms, stomachs and legs, but there are no universal rules. Some cover their arms; others do not. Hair sometimes shows at the back of headscarves. Face-veiling is extremely rare.

At some point, often in high school or college, girls transition from not wearing the veil to wearing one. For those who follow fashion trends before veiling, it is natural that they try to maintain their personal style when deciding how to veil. For others, such as fashion blogger Rania, a new interest in fashion coincides with covering. Over coffee at Am Plaz, a glitzy mall in Yogyakarta, Rania confided to me, 'Before I covered I thought that people who were into fashion were materialistic.' She continued, 'But when I started to wear *jilbab* I realized that I didn't have anything to wear except t-shirts and jeans and so I searched the internet for styles. For me, *jilbab* was a fashion opportunity.'

Today there is an enormous range of veiling options in Indonesia. Women can buy sporty, business, or formal ready-to-wear *jilbab*; hip to ankle length tunics; long pants, flowing skirts, or jeans; or 'regular' clothing, like strappy dresses, to wear over leggings and tight long-sleeved t-shirts called *manset*. When I was in Indonesia in 2011, trends in Islamic dress included tie-dyed fabrics, light pastel flowing cardigans, tops with dolman sleeves, and baggy harem pants with yards of fabric gathered at the knees or ankles (see figure 10, p. 142).

But by far the most attention is given to selecting and styling the focal point of Islamic dress: a headscarf. Again there are many options such as close-fitting or loose headscarves, pinned under the chin or not. Particularly in vogue in 2011 were 'ninja *ciputs*', tight base layers, worn under a voluminous pashmina shawl. Pamphlets and short books that give practical advice about types and styles help women select a headscarf. This advice literature, which has its own section in major bookstores like Gramedia (see figure 11, p. 144), gives step-by-step instructions for wrapping, twisting, and pinning headscarves to create different forms; advice about 'starter kits' that women should buy, such as the number and color of pins, brooches, *ciput*, and scarves; recommendations for how to match the pattern and color of a headscarf to the rest of the outfit; and guidelines for how to choose a

Figure 10 Veiling fashionistas in Am Plaz Mall, Yogyakarta, Indonesia

style, emphasizing the importance of wearing the veil in a flattering way. For instance, women with round or square faces are warned to be careful when choosing a style of head covering:

> Avoid wearing headscarves or base layers that cover the forehead because they will give the impression that the face is shorter. Avoid wearing a headscarf in the style that is pinned on the back of your neck because it will emphasize the chin and the jaw. It is better to wear visor *ciput* [a base layer with a built-in brim] with a wide visor that covers the ears so that it will give the impression that the face is longer and oval. (Author's translation, Rahmadini and Arsminda 2011, 6)

Indonesian women's quest to find a flattering veiling style raises an interesting question: is there a conflict between dressing fashionably and Islamic dressing? In other words, can or should wearing an Islamic veil actually increase the beauty of the woman? And if it does, is this in conflict with the veil's legal mandate to prevent *fitna* (sexual disorder) by covering a woman's 'awra ('vulnerable' body parts)? Or even worst, as the veil becomes a fashion trend in and of itself, is false veiling possible, where women choose to veil only because it is trendy?

Since the veil is so popular in Indonesia, some women do wear it merely as a fashion statement. This may seem surprising to some readers for whom the veil is laden with political and religious meanings. However the veil is not 'pregnant with meanings' in Indonesia to the same extent as it is in the US, Europe, and Middle East, for a variety of reasons. Although the majority of Indonesians are Muslim, veiling is not a symbol of the level of religiosity of a woman. You cannot tell if a woman prays five times a day by whether or not she veils. Veiling does not have the same loaded political history in Indonesia as it does in countries like Iran, Algeria, or Egypt where it has been used in political debates by both Islamists and secularists. Opposed to just ten

Figure 11 Veiling advice literature on sale at Gramedia bookstore, Yogyakarta, Indonesia

years ago when veiling was considered 'out of fashion', today it is 'in'. For women who wear a head covering only occasionally as a fashion statement, it is the 'look' of a headscarf, its color and pattern, its drape or volume, which motivates this fashion decision. It might simply be that a particular outfit is 'more fashionable' with a headscarf than without. In other words, in places where prevalent clothing trends cast the Islamic veil as 'in the mode', the veil may be worn primarily for its aesthetic value.

This sort of trend veiling is increasingly criticized in Indonesia, sometimes publicly, by Islamic vigilante groups who harass women from wearing what they deem to be false veiling, but more often privately by other Muslim women. However, for the most part fashionable veiling is tolerated in Indonesia, in part because what counts as beauty, as well as its relationship to fashion, is currently being recrafted to mean something more than 'superficial' appearance. For example, in the introduction to an Indonesian advice book, *60 Kesalahan Dalam Berjilbab* (*60 Common Veiling Mistakes*), authors Idatul Fitri and Nurul Khasanah differentiate between two sources of a woman's attractiveness and beauty, 'namely the physical beauty and inner beauty, or the beauty that comes from the inside'. Outer beauty 'can be seen in the face, manner of dress, and the body', while inner beauty 'can be seen from the way she behaves, talks, and also her polite, soft, and proper words' (author's translation, Fitri and Khasanah 2011, vii). It is clear that physical beauty alone is not the goal for a good Muslim woman, but rather cultivating a deeper, inner beauty that is connected to her virtue. But it is also clear that the two are not unrelated. As another Indonesian advice publication declares, 'when that inner beauty is surrounded by beautiful designs, it can radiate even more' (translated by Jones 2010, 105). In other words, outer beauty can intensify inner beauty, at least for the observer.

This concept of inner beauty is doing substantial theological work, even if, as in the case of the Iranian *bad hijab* girls, this work is unintentional. First, implicit in the valorization of beauty is a reference to Islamic principles of cleanliness. Thus fashion is recast as self-grooming for Allah. This allows beauty, even outer beauty, to be reclaimed as a positive norm: it is distinguished from individualistic attempts to gain sexual attention by linking beauty to obedience to God's plan.

Second, the linking of outer and inner beauty connects ethics and aesthetics in an intimate way, so that Islamic dress can pursue both ends. Fashion is not a litmus test for morality, but it does 'realign image and substance in a morally true order' (Jones 2010, 106) so that there is no conflict between being and looking good.

Third, this view of beauty also helps us to understand how Indonesians define the requirements of Islamic dress. In the discussion of the Qur'anic duty to veil in chapter 2 we saw that the meaning of the veil depends on the manner in which the interpreter defines *zina*, or what aspects of women's beauty must be covered. In Indonesia, *zina* is defined loosely as hair, legs, shoulders, and arms and the objective to cover is taken literally as 'cover with cloth'. For example, most Indonesians don't think it is necessary to cover a woman's shape: tight *mansets*, belts, even leggings are common. That a woman would and should find a fashion style that makes her more beautiful, even flattering her figure, is accepted and even expected. In other words, 'adornment' is made permissible, even desirable, by severing it from *zina*.

Evolving South Indian conceptions of modesty

Looking at the specific forms of dress Muslim women use helps to explain how even what comprises modesty differs cross-culturally. For example, in the case of Iran described earlier, the authorities are concerned with *bad hijab* because it includes *manteaus* that are tight and flashy: while physically covering a woman's body, they accentuate a woman's form. In Iran, local norms of modesty are connected to hiding a woman's shape. In Indonesia, however, tight undergarments, such as *manset*, are not seen as violations of modesty, nor are belts that cinch tightly at a woman's waist. In the Indonesian context, modesty is about literally covering a woman's skin and hair, not disguising her figure. It is very common in North America to see young veiled woman wearing tight skinny jeans or leggings with a t-shirt. In these cases, modesty is enacted by covering the hair and the rest of the body is freely displayed. In these ways, the diversity of Muslim fashion allows us to see that modesty and decency are not universal norms.

In South Asian contexts, the Islamic veil is part of a larger system of complex rules of modesty and gender seclusion referred to as *purdah*. *Purdah* is achieved through gender segregation and covering of women. It 'is an important part of the life experience of many South Asians, both Muslim and Hindu, and is a central feature of the social system in the area. The crucial characteristic of the *purdah* system is its limitation on interaction between women and males outside certain well defined categories' (Papanek 1973, 289). *Purdah* restrictions differ among Muslims and Hindus both in terms of when they begin (at puberty for Muslims and with marriage for Hindus) and to whom they apply (Muslims do not follow *purdah* restrictions in front of immediate family, but for Hindus, *purdah* applies to interactions with in-laws of the opposite sex). Typically *purdah* has been practised in North India, although increasingly women throughout India follow *purdah*.

Indian styles of women's dress have shifted since the nineteenth century. However, throughout the twentieth century, the sari gradually replaced other forms of dress as the pan-South

Asian female garment (Banerjee & Miller 2003). The now iconic sari is a six-meter piece of cloth, draped around the body. It is worn with a floor-length under-skirt and a blouse. Until the 1980s it was by far the most popular form of dress among both Hindu and Muslim South Indian women, both for everyday wear, as well as formal occasions such as weddings. In contrast to other areas of South Asia, South Indian women for the most part did not adopt European-style shirt, skirt, or trousers, which in this region still 'carry the slight smack of [licentiousness] and immodesty' (Osella & Osella 2007, 236).

In the 1980s, Hindus and Muslims developed significantly different sartorial practices related to the sari. For the most part, Hindus continued to pair the sari with a short tight blouse that exposes the midriff and most of the arm. Even older Hindu women continue to expose a great deal of skin while wearing their 'modest' saris and wear large groupings of jewelry such as bangles layered up the forearm. Young Hindu women wear waist-chains at the belly-button level. Up until the 1980s this form of sari-dress was seen as quintessentially Indian and fulfilling *purdah* restrictions for Hindus and Muslims.

However, a different logic of modesty and dress began to surface among South Indian Muslims in the 1980s. Influenced by global styles of Islamic dress, in which only the face, hands and feet are shown, South Indian Muslims began to see the sari style described above as reflecting the norms of dominant high-caste Hindus, instead of conveying pan-South Asian, Indian, or South Indian identity. South Indian Muslims began to wear long-sleeved blouses under their saris, and added separately purchased head-scarves (Osella and Osella 2007, 237). They also adopted new styles of dress, for example, *salwaar kameez*, a long tunic over pants worn with a coordinating shawl. By the 1990s this became the preferred style of dress for many South Indian Muslims, because it did not reveal or accentuate female bodies nor was it perceived as an explicit Hindu cultural form like the sari. In contrast, South Indian Hindus criticized *salwaar kameez* as the importation of north Indian and Pakistani cultural norms. Some Hindus also found the pants to be immodest.

One result of recent Gulf migration to India has been the proliferation of the Gulf style of dress called *abaya*. In Kerala, 'women under thirty tend to prefer this sophisticated garment', Caroline and Filippo Osella write, because it is form-fitting, while 'those who are more matronly choose the looser and less conspicuous' local versions such as a sari or *salwaar kameez* (Osella & Osella 2007, 243). Karen Ruffle, who conducts research on Shi'i ritual and gender in Hyderabad, has also observed a recent local shift from sari to *abaya*. She notes that *abaya* is particularly popular among young Shi'i women, while it is more typical to see older Shi'i women in a sari with a small floral *chador* draped loosely over the head and shoulders (correspondence with author 2011).

These variations in sartorial practices reflect Hindu and Muslim South Indians' different understandings of female modesty and thus what comprises decent dress. Based on several periods of fieldwork in Kerala, Osella and Osella conclude that 'for Hindu women, modesty is about wrapping, restraining and binding: clothes are tight, wound around the body, and jewelry such as anklets and bangles contain the bodily extremities' (Osella & Osella 2007, 236). Thus when Hindu women ask tailors to make their blouse sleeves as tight as possible this is out of obedience, not resistance, to decency norms. In contrast, most South Indian Muslims now style their sari, *salwaar kameez*, or *abaya* so that the body is not revealed. For them, tight clothing is no longer appropriate or able to convey modesty. Thus, tight blouses or exposed midriffs are part of how South Indian Hindus maintain *purdah*, but for South India Muslims, these satorial practices are violations of *purdah*.

Summary

This chapter has described the influence of fashion on the Islamic veil. Practically, fashion affects what Muslim women wear. conceptually, reconciling fashion and Islam affects the interpretation and implementation of Islamic principles related to veiling, such as what is proper *hijab*? What must be covered by it? Can a woman be both stylish and fulfill Islamic norms associated with veiling?

A couple of general points have been argued. First, everyday practices, such as fashion-veiling, can contribute to and shift religious traditions. The way young girls style their Islamic dress in Iran has changed the enforcement of Shari'a law in that context by making what used to be *bad hijab* (exposed ankles, peeking fringes) seem moderate. *Hijabi* fashionistas in Indonesia are affecting Islam locally by defining a new moral role for women's adornment and beauty. When young South Indian Muslims adopt Pakistani (*salwaar kameez*) or Gulf (*abaya*) forms of modest dress, they establish and reinforce a specific understanding of what counts as modesty against dominant Hindu norms. In this chapter, we have glimpsed the power of practice through the impact of fashion, which is not only an issue of aesthetics, but also of theological and ethical domains of religious belief and practice.

Second, part of the importance of fashion to veiling is how the production and marketing of clothing is shaping certain types of Muslim subjects, specifically women who want to look a certain way (be fashionable) while fulfilling their duty to cover. While there are some vocal critics within, and outside, the Muslim community, who judge fashion-veiling to be superficial and in conflict with the goals of modest dress, for the most part fashionable, beautiful veiling is admired. Creating an outer and inner beauty, a pious and modern appearance, requires resourcefulness and skill. It is achieved through mastery of the unspoken rules of wearing gendered Islamic dress.

Conclusion

In many ways, this book is an introduction to the invention of the modern Islamic veil. By invention I do not mean 'to make up something false', or even 'make up something completely new', that is, without historical or doctrinal precedent, but rather, 'to produce through experimentation'. In the case of the Islamic veil, this production takes place within everyday cultural and social experiences and is the work not only of Muslim scholars, but also ordinary Muslim believers as well as non-Muslims. Qur'anic commentators, for example, invent the veil when they read three distinct cases of revelation together (see chapter 2). Legal scholars invent the veil through connecting of women's bodies to worldly disorder (see chapter 3). In the modern world, human experiences with colonialism, employment, education, identity, and fashion reinvent the Islamic veil when individuals, communities, and nations adopt it for specific agendas (see chapters 4, 5, 6, 7, and 8). The veil as an object, concept, and ideology is reified and reinscribed every time it is used. This means that what the veil was may not reflect what it has come to be in the contemporary world. For example, even if the veil was not required by seventh-century revelations, as recorded in the Qur'an or hadith, it may serve a purpose today as modern Muslim women are increasingly required to participate in public life.

Throughout this book, I have used regional case studies to demonstrate the manner in which various dimensions of the Islamic veil are made concrete, thus showing how the veil obtained enormous regional diversity. The compulsory veil of Saudi Arabia, for instance, is not the same as the post-Soviet veil in Tajikistan, nor the Turkish veil in universities, nor the Indonesian fashion-veil. Every geographic and historic context has its own set of rich and complex meanings and tangible nuanced forms.

As such a complex cluster of practices, discourses, and politics, the Islamic veil inevitably entails internal tensions and paradoxes, and thus leaves room for disagreement. For some, the veil is a signifier of women's oppression by men, but for others it is a feminist choice. In classical thought, the veil's purpose is to protect women from the male gaze, and yet in contemporary practice it often increases the visibility of Muslim women, especially those in Muslim minority settings. Paradoxes even occur within the same specific instance of veiling. A veiled working-woman, for example, may find herself simultaneously affirming the values of both gender equality and sexual segregation. A woman may claim the veil prevents her from being objectified as a woman, yet find herself objectified as a fundamentalist once she puts on the veil.

Feminism revisited: lessons from the comparative study of the veil

In the introduction I shared my own early ignorance about the Islamic veil that became clear to me during fieldwork in Iran. I can now see how those initial misunderstandings came from my prior feminist political commitments. Since I do not normally veil, and live in a country in which veiling is optional, the require-ment of all women in Iran to veil seemed to me a violation of their freedom. I expected Iranian women to behave as I would in the same situation: throwing off the veil, or resisting it in subver-sive ways. My own political agenda affected my ability to see the other dimensions of the veil.

If we can see the veil in a new light, however, it can help us to rethink feminism, particularly the importance of making a distinction between feminist description, feminist explanation, and feminist politics. Feminist description seeks to provide details of women's lives. In the case of the Islamic veil, feminist description is concerned with the actual forms of dress women wear and the circumstances under which these forms change. Feminist explanation goes a step further, attempting to explain why Muslim women veil in the first place. Feminist politics is the most normative of the group. It often begins with assumptions about women's constrained freedom under conditions of patriarchy and a desire to eradicate these conditions. In other words, feminist politics begins with a normative claim (women are equal to men) and a rebellious agenda (women must be treated as equal to men). Feminist politics then is acutely concerned with critique and reform. In the case of the Islamic veil, feminist politics might attempt to assess this practice as either part of women's subordination or their freedom.

The Islamic veil raises an important challenge to the proper role of feminist politics in comparative studies. The range of actual practices of the veil in the contemporary world complicates any attempt to judge it as universally good or bad. It is used in a variety of ways: as a fashion statement, to run for political office, to obtain an education, to express cultural identity. In other words, the Islamic veil is used to participate in many dimensions of public life and in each of these cases the meaning, perception, and power of the veil is different. In order to make any moral judgment about the veil we must specify to which form of practice we are referring, by which women, before which audience, within which historical or cultural context, and for which end.

A final word of caution

There is nothing necessarily more 'natural' about blue jeans and a t-shirt than a headscarf, *manteau*, or *burqa*, even if one is more accustomed to looking at the former. Each occupies an interested space. Each does political work. All human dress speaks of social order and, therefore, is never politically or morally neutral. Add religion to the mix, and forms of religious dress become even more difficult to understand. Given the global debates surrounding veiling practices in various communities, we might do well to remember that judgment of another's dress privileges our own cultural context, and that this is often done to the detriment of understanding the diversity of ways of life. For instance, there is a tendency in Western media to present the use of high heels and cosmetics as evidence for the increased liberation of women in Muslim majority societies. We applaud beauty salons in Kabul. We call makeup in Tehran a lipstick jihad. But we should be cautious of how easily this becomes 'cultural colonialism'. In this rhetoric, stilettos are a sign of 'liberation' not because they mean women are becoming more liberated, but rather that they are becoming more like Western women. This is not necessarily the same thing.

Further reading

Introduction

Abu-Lughod, L. 2002. 'Do Muslim Women Really Need Saving? Anthropological Reflections on Cultural Relativism and Its Others', *American Anthropologist* 104, no. 3, pp. 783–790.

Ahmed, A. 2011. *A Quiet Revolution: The Veil's Resurgence, from the Middle East to America*. New Haven, Yale University Press.

Alvi, S.S., Hoodfar, H. & McDonough, S. ed. 2003. *The Muslim Veil in North America*. Toronto, Women's Press.

Hirschmann, N. 1997. 'Eastern Veiling, Western Freedom?' *The Review of Politics* 59, no. 3, pp. 461–488.

Said, E. W. 1979. *Orientalism*. New York, Vintage Books.

1 Ethics

Ali, K. 2006. *Sexual Ethics and Islam: Feminist Reflections on Qur'ran, Hadith, and Jurisprudence*. Oxford, Oneworld Publications.

Hashimi. S., ed. 2002. *Islamic Political Ethics: Civil Society, Pluralism, and Conflict*. Princeton, Princeton University Press.

Mahmmod, S. 2004. *Politics of Piety: The Islamic Revival and the Feminist Subject*. Princeton, Princeton University Press.

Moosa, E. 2005. 'Muslim ?' in *The Blackwell Companion to Religious Ethics*, ed. W. Schweiker. Oxford, Blackwell.

2 Sacred texts

Clarke, L. 2003. '*Hijab* According to the *Hadith*: Text and Interpretation', in *The Muslim Veil in North America*, ed. S.S. Alvi, H. Hoodfar, & S. McDonough, pp. 214–286. Toronto, Women's Press.

Goto, E. 2004. 'Qur'an and the Veil: Contexts and Interpretations of the Revelation', *International Journal of Asian Studies* 1, no. 2, pp. 277–295.

Hajjaji-Jarrah, S. 2003. 'Women's Modesty in Qur'anic Commentaries: The Founding Discourse', in *The Muslim Veil in North America*, ed. S.S. Alvi, H. Hoodfar, & S. McDonough, pp 181–213. Toronto, Women's Press.

Hoffman, V.J. 1998. 'Qur'anic Interpretation and Modesty' in *The Shaping of an American Islamic Discourse: A Memorial to Fazlur Rhaman*, ed. E. Waugh and F. Denny, pp. 89–121. Atlanta, Scholars Press.

Mernissi, F. 1991. *The Veil and the Male Elite*, trans. M.J. Lakeland. Reading, Perseus Books.

Stowasser, B.F. 1994. *Women in the Qur'an, Traditions, and Interpretation*. New York, Oxford University Press.

Wadud, A. 1999. *Qur'an and Woman: Rereading the Sacred Text from a Woman's Perspective*. New York, Oxford University Press.

3 Law

Ali, K. 2010. *Marriage and Slavery in Early Islam*. Cambridge, Harvard University Press.

El Fadl, A. 2001. *Speaking in God's Name: Islamic Law, Authority and Women*. Oxford, Oneworld.

Hallaq, W.B. 1984. 'Was the Gate of Ijtihad Closed?' *International Journal of Middle East Studies* 16, no. 1, pp. 3–41.

Reinhart, K.A. 1983. 'Islamic Law as Islamic Ethics', *Journal of Religious Ethics* 11, no. 2, pp. 186–203.

Tucker, J. 1998. *In the House of the Law: Gender and Islamic Law in Ottoman Syria and Palestine*. Berkeley, University of California Press.

Tucker, J. 2008. *Women, Family, and Gender in Islamic Law*. Cambridge, Cambridge University Press.

4 Colonialism

Ahmed, L. 1992. *Women and Gender in Islam*. New Haven, Yale University Press.

Amin, Q. 2000. *The Liberation of Women and The New Woman: Two Documents in the History of Egyptian Feminism*, trans. S.S. Peterson. Cairo, The American University of Cairo Press.

Badran, M. 1995. *Feminists, Islam, and Nation: Gender and the Making of Modern Egypt*. Princeton, Princeton University Press.

Fanon, F. 1965. *A Dying Colonialism*, trans. H. Chevalier & intro. A. Gilly. New York, Grove Press.

Hammami, R. 1990. 'Women, the Hijab and the Intifada', *Middle East Report*, 164/165, pp. 24–28, 71, 78.

Lazreg, M. 1990. 'Gender and Politics in Algeria: Unraveling the Religious Paradigm', *Signs*, 15, no. 4, pp. 755–780.

Loomba, A. 2005. *Colonialism/Postcolonialism*, second edition. New York, Routledge.

5 Employment

Hoodfar, H. 1997. *Between Marriage and the Market: Intimate Politics and Survival In Cairo*. Berkeley, University of California Press.

Lemmon, G.T. 2011. *The Dressmaker of Khair Khana: Five Sisters, One Remarkable Family, and the Woman Who Risked Everything to Keep Them Safe*. New York, HarperCollins Publishers.

MacLeod, A.E. 1991. *Accommodating Protest: Working Women, the New Veiling, and Change in Cairo*. New York, Columbia University Press.

6 Education

Bowen, J.R. 2007. *Why the French Don't Like Headscarves*. Princeton, Princeton University Press.

Göle, N. 1997. *The Forbidden Modern: Civilization and Veiling*. Ann Arbor, University of Michigan Press.

Hefner-Smith, N. 2007. 'Muslim Women and the Veil in Post-Soeharto Java', *Journal of Asian Studies*, 66, no. 22, pp. 389–420.

Leyla Sahin v. Turkey. 2005. Application no. 44774/98. Judgment 10 November 2005. Strasbourg, European Court of Human Rights.

Scott, J.W. 2007. *Politics of the Veil*. Princeton, Princeton University Press.

Najmabadi, A. 2006. 'Gender and secularism of modernity: How can a Muslim woman be French?' *Feminist Studies* 32, no. 2, pp. 239–255.

7 Identity

Heath, J., ed. 2008. *The Veil: Women Writers on Its History, Lore, and Politics*. Berkeley, University of California Press, 2008.

Lazreg, M. 2009. *Questioning the Veil: Open Letters to Muslim Women*. Princeton, Princeton University Press.

Moghadam, V.M. 1994. 'Purdah provides the Opportunity for Preserving One's Own Identity and a Certain Stability in the Face of External Pressures', in *Gender and National Identity*, ed. V.M. Moghadam. Atlantic Highlands, Zed Books Ltd.

8 Fashion

Balasescu, A. 2007. 'Haute Couture in Tehran: Two faces of an emerging fashion scene', *Fashion Theory*, 11, pp. 299–318.

Gökariksel, B. & A. Secor. 2010. 'Between Fashion and Tesettür: Marketing and Consuming Women's Islamic Dress', *Journal of Middle East Women's Studies*, 6, no. 3, pp. 118–148.

Jones, C. 2010. 'Images of Desire: Creating Virtue and Value in an Indonesian Islamic Lifestyle Magazine', *Journal of Middle East Women's Studies*, 6, no. 3, pp. 91–117.

Niessen, S., Leshkowich, A., and Jones, C. *Re-Orienting Fashion: The Globalization of Asian Dress*, pp. 243–266. Oxford, Berg.

Osello, C. & F. Osello. 2007. 'Muslim Style in South India', *Fashion Theory*, 11, no. 2/3, pp. 233–252.

Tarlo, E. 2010. *Visbly Muslim: Fashion, Politics, Faith*. Oxford, Berg.

Bibliography

Abu-Lughod, L., ed. 1998. *Remaking Women: Feminism and Modernity in the Middle East*. Princeton, Princeton University Press.

Ahmed, L. 1992. *Women and Gender in Islam*. New Haven, Yale University Press.

_____. 2011. *A Quiet Revolution: The Veil's Resurgence, from the Middle East to America*. New Haven, Yale University Press.

Ali, A.Y., trans. 26th US edition 2010. *The Qur'an: Translation*. ed. S. Smith. New York, Tahrike Tarsile Qur'an, Inc.

Ali, K. 2006. *Sexual Ethics and Islam: Feminist Reflections on Qur'ran, Hadith, and Jurisprudence*. Oxford, Oneworld Publications.

_____. 2010. *Marriage and Slavery in Early Islam*. Cambridge, Harvard University Press.

Althusser, L. 1971. *Lenin and Philosophy and Other Essays*, trans. B. Brewster. New York, Monthly Review Press.

Amin, Q. 2000. *The Liberation of Women and the New Woman: Two Documents in the History of Egyptian Feminism*, trans. S.S. Peterson. New York, The American University of Cairo Press.

AOL News. 2010. 'Store Fires Woman for Wearing Muslim Head Scarf', aolnews.com, 26 February, viewed 8 August 2011, www.aolnews.com.

Arberry, A.J. 1996. *The Koran Interpreted*. New York, Simon & Schuster.

Badran, M. 1995. *Feminists, Islam, and Nation: Gender and the Making of Modern Egypt*. Princeton, Princeton University Press.

Bahramitash, R. 2002. 'Islamic Fundamentalism and Women's Employment in Indonesia', *International Journal of Politics*, 16, no. 2, pp. 255–272.

Balasescu, A. 2007. 'Haute Couture in Tehran: Two faces of an emerging fashion scene', *Fashion Theory*, 11, pp. 299–318.

Banerjee, M. & Miller, D. 2003. *The Sari*. Oxford, Berg Publications.

Bly, L. 2010. 'Hostess accuses Disney of dress-code discrimination; Muslim woman says she was told she couldn't wear hijab at work', *USA Today*, 27 August, p. 10B.

Boellstorff, T. 2004. 'Playing Back the Nation: *Waria*, Indonesian Transvestites', *Cultural Anthropology*, 19, no. 2, pp. 159–195.

al-Bukhari, M. 1976–79. *The Translation of the Meanings of Sahih al-Bukhari*, trans. M. M. Khan. 9 vols. Chicago, Kaze Publications.

Clarke, L. 2003. '*Hijab* According to the *Hadith*: Text and Interpretation', in *The Muslim Veil in North America*, ed. S.S. Alvi, H. Hoodfar, & S. McDonough, pp. 214–286. Toronto, Women's Press.

Cole, J.R.I. & D. Kandiyoti. 2002. 'Nationalism and the Colonial Legacy in the Middle East and Central Asia: Introduction', *International Journal of Middle East Studies* 34, no. 2, pp. 189–203.

Dass, N. 2002. 'Afghanistan-Human Right', in *Encyclopedia of Modern Asia*, ed. K. Christensen & D. Levinson, vol. 1, pp. 25–27. New York, Charles Scribner's Sons.

Dawood, N.J., trans. 2006. *The Koran: With A Parallel Arabic Text*. London, Penguin.

Dillon, M. 1999. *Catholic Identity: Balancing Reason, Faith, and Power*. New York, Cambridge University Press.

European Court of Human Rights. 2008. 'Press release issued by the Registrar; Two Chamber judgments in respect of France on wearing the headscarf in school', 4 December 2008, viewed on 8 August 2010, http://echr.coe.int/echr/en/hudoc.

El Fadl, A. 2001. *Speaking in God's Name: Islamic Law, Authority and Women*. Oxford, Oneworld.

Fanon, F. 1965. *A Dying Colonialism*, trans. H. Chevalier & intro. A. Gilly. New York, Grove Press.

Fitri, I. & Nurual K. 2011. *60 Kesalahan Dalam Berjilbab* (60 Common Veiling Mistakes). Jakarta, Basmallah.

Foucault, M. 1990. *The Use of Pleasure*. Vol. 2 of *The History of Sexuality*, trans. R. Hurley. New York, Vintage Books.

Gökariksel, B. & A. Secor. 2009. 'New Transnational Geographies of Islamism, Capitalism, and Subjectivity: The Veiling-fashion Industry in Turkey', *Area*, 41, pp. 6–18.

_____. 2010a. 'Islamic-ness in the Life of a Commodity: Veiling-fashion in Turkey', *Transactions of the Institute of British Geographers*, 35, pp. 313–333.

_____. 2010b. 'Between Fashion and Tesettür: Marketing and Consuming Women's Islamic Dress', *Journal of Middle East Women's Studies*, 6, no. 3, pp. 118–148.

Göle, N. 1997. *The Forbidden Modern: Civilization and Veiling*. Ann Arbor, University of Michigan Press.

_____. 2003. 'The Voluntary Adoption of Islamic Stigma Symbols', *Social Research*, 70, no. 3, pp. 809–828.

Gordon, D.G. 1962. *Women in Algeria: An Essay on Change*. Cambridge, Harvard University Press.

Goto, E. 2004. 'Qur'an and the Veil: Contexts and Interpretations of the Revelation', *International Journal of Asian Studies*, 1, no. 2, pp. 277–295.

Greenhouse, S. 2010. 'U.S. Muslims ill at ease on the job: Complaints of hostility in the workplace jump 60% over 4 years', *The International Herald Tribune*, 24 September, p. 17.

El Guindi, F. 1999. *Veil: Modesty, Privacy and Resistance*. Oxford, Berg.

_____. 2005. 'Gendered Resistance, Feminist Veiling, Islamic Feminism', *The Ahfad Journal*, 22, no. 1, pp. 53–78.

Haddad, Y.Y. 2007. 'The Post-9/11 *Hijab* as Icon', *Sociology of Religion*, 68, no. 3, pp. 253–267.

Hadot, P. 1995. *Philosophy as a Way of Life: Spiritual Exercises from Socrates to Foucault*, ed. A. Davidson, trans. M. Chase. Oxford, Blackwell.

Hajjaji-Jarrah, S. 2003. 'Women's Modesty in Qur'anic Commentaries: The Founding Discourse', in *The Muslim Veil in North America*, ed. S.S. Alvi, H. Hoodfar, & S. McDonough, pp. 181–213. Toronto, Women's Press.

Hallaq, W.B. 1984. 'Was the Gate of Ijtihad Closed?' *International Journal of Middle East Studies*, 16, no. 1, pp. 3–41.

Hammami, R. 1990. 'Women, the Hijab and the Intifada', *Middle East Report*, 164/165, pp. 24–28,71,78.

Hashmi, S.H., ed. 2002. *Islamic Political Ethics: Civil Society, Pluralism, and Conflict*. Princeton, Princeton University Press.

Haw, K. 2009. 'From Hijab to Jilbab and the "Myth" of British Identity: Being Muslim in Contemporary Britain a Half-generation on', *Race Ethnicity and Education*, 12, no. 3, pp. 363–378.

Hizb ut-Tahrir. 2003. 'The Attack on the Veil', *Khilafah Magazine*, 16, no. 7, pp. 19–21.

Hoodfar, H. 1997. *Between Marriage and the Market: Intimate Politics and Survival in Cairo*. Berkeley, University of California Press.

Human Rights Watch. 2004. 'Memorandum to the Turkish Government on Human Rights Watch's Concerns with Regard to Academic Freedom in Higher Education, and Access to Higher Education for Women who Wear the Headscarf', June 29 2004, viewed on 8 August 2011, http://www.hrw.org.

_____. 2005. 'Turkey; Headscarf Ruling Denies Women Education and Career', 15 November 2005 viewed on 8 August 2011, http://www. hrw.org.

Ibn Khaldun. 1958. *The Muqaddimah: An Introduction to History*, trans. F. Rosenthal. New York, Pantheon Books.

Iranian Constitution. 1979. Adopted 24 October 1979, viewed 8 August 2011, http://www.iranonline.com.

Islamic Penal Code of Iran. 1996. Ratified 22 May 1996, viewed 8 August 2011, http://www.unhcr.org.

Jones, C. 2010. 'Images of Desire: Creating Virtue and Value in an Indonesian Islamic Lifestyle Magazine', *Journal of Middle East Women's Studies*, 6, no. 3, pp. 91–117.

_____. 2007. 'Fashion and Faith in Urban Indonesia', *Fashion Theory*, 11, no. 2/3, pp. 211–232.

Kazemi, F. 2002. 'Perspectives on Islam and Civil Society', *Islamic Political Ethics: Civil Society, Pluralism, and Conflict*, ed. S.H. Hashmi. Princeton, Princeton University Press.

Khalafallah, H. 2005. 'Muslim Women: Public Authority, Scriptures, and "Islamic Law" ', in *Beyond the Exotic: Women's Histories in Islamic Societies*, ed. A.E.A. Sonbol. Syracuse, Syracuse University Press.

Khalidi, R. 1997. *Palestinian Identity: The Construction of Modern National Consciousness*. New York, Columbia University Press.

Khomeini, R. 1978. *The Position of Women From the Viewpoint of Imam Khomeini*, trans. J. Shaw & B. Arezoo. Tehran, The Institute for Compilation and Publication of Imam Khomeini's Works.

Lazreg, M. 1990. 'Gender and Politics in Algeria: Unraveling the Religious Paradigm', *Signs*, 15, no. 4, pp. 755–780.

_____. 2009. *Questioning the Veil: Open Letters to Muslim Women*. Princeton, Princeton University Press.

Lemmon, G.T. 2011. *The Dressmaker of Khair Khana: Five Sisters, One Remarkable Family, and the Woman Who Risked Everything to Keep Them Safe*. New York, HarperCollins Publishers.

Leyla Sahin v. Turkey. 2005. Application no. 44774/98. Judgment 10 November 2005. Strasbourg, European Court of Human Rights.

Loomba, A. 2005. *Colonialism/Postcolonialism*, second edition. New York, Routledge.

MacLeod, A.E. 1991. *Accommodating Protest: Working Women, the New Veiling, and Change in Cairo*. New York, Columbia University Press.

_____. 1992. 'Hegemonic Relations and Gender Resistance: The New Veiling as Accommodating Protest in Cario', *Signs*, 17, no. 3, pp. 533–557.

Mahmood, S. 2001. 'Feminist Theory, Embodiment, and the Docile Agent: Some Reflections on the Egyptian Islamic Revival', *Cultural Anthropology*, 16, no. 2, pp. 202–236.

_____. 2005. *Politics of Piety: The Islamic Revival and the Feminist Subject*. Princeton, Princeton University Press.

Mamaraimov, A. & Asanova, S. No date. 'Headscarf Bans Remain Live Issues in Central Asia', Women Worldwide Advancing Freedom and Equality, viewed 8 August 2011, http://www.wafe-women.org.

Maududi, A. 1972 [1992 12th edition]. *Purdah and The Status of Women in Islam*, trans. Al-Ash'ari. Lahore, Islamic Publications Limited.

Mernissi, F. 1991. *The Veil and the Male Elite*, trans. M.J. Lakeland. Reading, Perseus Books.

Moazzam, A. 1984. *Jamal al-Din al-Afghani: A Muslim Intellectual*. New Delhi: Concept.

Mutahhari, M. 1992, 3rd edition. *The Islamic Modest Dress*, trans. L. Baktiar. Chicago, Kazi Publications.

Nabiyeva, D. 2011. 'Tajik Women Pressured to Wear Hijab', *CentralAsiaOnline.com*, 3 March 2011, viewed on 8 August 2011, http://centralasiaonline.com.

Niessen, S. 2003. 'Afterword: Re-Orienting Fashion Theory', in *Re-Orienting Fashion: The Globalization of Asian Dress*, ed. S. Niessen, A.M. Leshkowich, & C. Jones, pp. 243–266. Oxford, Berg.

Okkenhaug, I.M. & Flaskerud, I. 2005. *Gender, Religion and Change in the Middle East: Two Hundred Years of History*. Oxford, Berg.

Osello, C. & F. Osello, 2007. 'Muslim Style in South India', *Fashion Theory*, 11, no. 2/3, pp. 233–252.

Papanek, H. 1973. 'Purdah: Separate Worlds and Symbolic Shelter', *Comparative Studies in Society and History*, 15, no. 3, pp. 289–325.

Peek, L. 2005. 'Becoming Muslim: The Development of a Religious Identity', *Sociology of Religion*, 66, no. 3, pp. 215–242.

Pollitt, K. 2010. 'Veil of Fears', *The Nation*, 14 June, p. 10.

Rahmadini, K. & Arsminda, T. 2011. *Aneka Kreasi Kerudung Cantik: Gaya dasar memakai kerudung segi empat & selendang* (Various creations of beautiful headscarves: Basic styles of wearing square headscarf & rectangle headscarf). Jakarta, Demedia Pustaka.

Rashid, A. 2000. *Taliban: Militant Islam, Oil and Fundamentalism in Central Asia*. New Haven, Yale Nota Bene Books.

Rasmussen, S.J. 2010. 'The Slippery Sign: Cultural Constructions of Youth and Youthful Constructions of Culture in Tuareg Men's Face Veiling', *Journal of Anthropological Research*, 66, pp. 463–484.

Said, E.W. 1979. *Orientalism*. New York, Vintage Books.

Schulz, D.E. 2007. 'Competing Sartorial Assertions of Femininity and Muslim Identity in Mali', *Fashion Theory*, 11, no. 2/3, pp. 253–280.

Scott, J.W. 2007. *Politics of the Veil*. Princeton, Princeton University Press.

Shirazi, F. 2001. *The Veil Unveiled: The Hijab in Modern Culture*. Tallahassee, University of Florida Press.

Shipler, D.M. 2002. *Arab and Jew: Wounded Spirits in a Promised Land*. New York, Penguin Group.

Smith-Hefner, N.J. 2007. 'Javanese Women and the Veil in Post-Soeharto Indonesia', *The Journal of Asian Studies*, 66, no. 2, pp. 389–420.

Stowasser, B.F. 1994. *Women in the Qur'an, Traditions, and Interpretation*. New York, Oxford University Press.

Straw, J. 2006. 'I want to unveil my views on an important issue', *Lancashire Telegraph*, 6 October.

Stryker, S. 1980. *Symbolic Interactionism: A Social Structural Version*. Menlo Park, Benjamin/Cummings.

Tarlo, E. 2010. *Visbly Muslim: Fashion, Politics, Faith*. Oxford, Berg.

Taylor, P. 2008. 'I Just Want to Be Me: Issues of Identity for One American Muslim Woman', in *The Veil: Women Writers on Its History, Lore, and Politics*, ed. J. Heath, pp. 119–136. Berkeley, University of California Press.

Telesetsky, A. 1998. 'In the Shadows and Behind the Veil: Women in Afghanistan Under Taliban Rule', *Berkeley Women's Law Journal*, 13, pp. 293–305.

de Tocqueville, A. 1954. 'Letter to J S Mill, 18 March 1841', in *Oeuvres complètes*, 'Correspondance anglaise', vol. 6, 1, Gallimard, Paris, p. 335.

Tucker, J. 2008. *Women, Family, and Gender in Islamic Law*. Cambridge, Cambridge University Press.

Vojdik, V. K. 2010. 'Politics of the Headscarf in Turkey: Masculinities, Feminism, and the Construction of Collective Identities', *Harvard Journal of Law and Gender*, 33, pp. 661–685.

Wadud, A. 1999. *Qur'an and Woman: Rereading the Sacred Text from a Woman's Perspective.* New York, Oxford University Press.

Warburton, E. 2008. 'Regulating Morality: Compulsory Veiling at an Indonesian University.' presented at the 19th Biennial Conference of the Asian Studies Association of Australia in Melbourne. July 1–3, viewed 8 August 2011, http://arts.monash.edu.au.

Zahedi, A. 2011. 'Muslim American Women in the Post-11 September Era', *International Feminist Journal of Politics*, 13, no. 2, pp. 183–203.

Index

Note: page numbers in bold denote illustrations